Changing the Way We Work

By the same author

The Coming Shape of Organization

How to Build a Successful Team ... the Belbin Way (CD-ROM)

The Job Promoters

Management Teams: Why They Succeed or Fail

Team Roles At Work

Changing the Way We Work

R. Meredith Belbin

Butterworth-Heinemann
Linacre House, Jordan Hill, Oxford OX2 8DP
A division of Reed Educational and Professional Publishing Ltd

℞ A member of the Reed Elsevier plc group

OXFORD   BOSTON   JOHANNESBURG
MELBOURNE   NEW DELHI   SINGAPORE

First published 1997

British Library Cataloguing in Publication Data
Belbin, R. M. (Raymond Meredith), 1926–
    Changing the Way We Work
    1. Industrial management   2. Delegation of authority
    I. Title
    658

ISBN 0 7506 2874 X

Composition by Genesis Typesetting, Laser Quay, Rochester, Kent
Printed and bound in Great Britain by Biddles Ltd,
Guildford and King's Lynn

Contents

List of colour plates   vii

Preface   ix

The colours of Workset   xi

1   Order and disorders   1
2   The true nature of a modern job   8
3   Reclassifying work: tasks versus responsibilities   16
4   'So what's the job?'   25
5   Overcoming initial problems   34
6   Job casting and job briefing   40
7   Improving communications   48
8   Quantifying the way we work   57
9   Managing the feedback   63
10   Creating a new culture   69
11   Fostering team empowerment   76
12   From competence to excellence   81
13   Team roles and colour codes   88
14   Managers and leaders revisited   94
15   A way forward   102

Appendix 1   A glossary of terms   108

Appendix 2   Workset – audit of existing practices in job setting   110

Index   114

Colour plates

Plate 1   The Workset cycle: adding colour and clarity to jobs

Plate 2   The job as viewed from two positions

Plate 3   The dynamic nature of a job

Plate 4   Prompting questions for dividing the work into sets

Plate 5   Contrasts in communication

Plate 6   Explanation of Workset colour sets

Plate 7   The dynamics of Workset: an interactive model

Plate 8   The skills focus of Workset

Preface

'What surprised me was the large amount of Green Work throughout the organization and there is much less Blue Work than we expected.' 'Yes, but the real shock is the extent of the Pink Work. This ought to be cut down and replaced with more Yellow Work.'

This typical sample of a seemingly cryptic conversation will be meaningful to the small numbers of people already familiar with Workset, which is a system of colour coding devised to improve communications about the nature and demands of jobs. More specifically, Workset has two aims: first, to enable jobholders and managers to speak more freely to one another in a language each can understand, once that language has been learned; and, second, to generate data that, in highlighting organizational weaknesses, will enable managers to take remedial action.

Few things start as though from nothing and this is true of the content of *Changing The Way We Work*, which is a continuation and expansion of a theme first introduced in *The Coming Shape of Organization*. That this new book should appear so shortly after the publication of my earlier book is testimony to the speed with which events can move once an idea has taken root. Yet there is also a downside which makes me feel as if constrained to write an interim book, constructed to cover some artificial segment of time carved out of a continuous process.

Every book needs a beginning and an end. All I would say about the beginning is that, if something can be traced to its source, I would mention Rosemary Stewart and her many writings about the jobs of managers, about the differences between core work and peripheral work and about the distinctive ways in which people interpret and manage their boundary areas; and the impression made upon me when I attended a course at the Durham Business School. It took some years for me to grasp how we could respond proactively to the challenge posed by some of the observed realities that were presented.

And, about the end, I would say there is no end, for we are now caught up in the busy pressures of the change process itself.

I have written this book in the conviction that many of the problems that arise at work are due to the way in which jobs are set up. People are uncertain about their responsibilities; they spend undue time and energy trying to sort out their personal duties and disentangling them from those of co-workers; they are overworked and underworked because the workload cannot be more equitably distributed; they strive to cope with the failure of others while struggling to avoid charges of intrusion. Or the very opposite conditions prevail: jobs are marked out like territories on a housing estate, where neighbours never mix, except for an exchange of conventional greetings, and boundaries, established by legal contract, are immutable. For the captains of industry the bleak choice often lies between dynamic chaos and lifeless bureaucracy.

But there is another route that beckons the navigator and which I have endeavoured to set out. The subject addressed in this book starts tentatively with some ideas; it proceeds under the stimulus of pilot studies and experiences in three countries – the UK, Australia and Sweden – and concludes at the time when sponsored trials are making good progress in Leicester Royal Infirmary, ICI at Wilton and US Airtours, while other trials await their turn.

These applications owe much to valued suggestions that have been made from time to time; in which connection I am grateful to John Burns from Australia, Christer Jansson and Inger Melkersson from Sweden, Rob Groen from Holland, Malcolm Yates and Mike Tanner from the UK, and, at a practical level especially, to Thomas Ekbom for his pilot work in the Swedish Prison Service. Others in industry, to whom I am indebted, were members of a team, so I will not single them out for mention; yet without the faith of these anonymous contributors that we were heading in at least a promising direction, the much-needed lessons of experience would never have been gained.

Finally I would like to record my thanks to my close colleague, Barrie Watson, for his energy, support and resourcefulness as a prime mover in getting things going in the UK, to Peter Lancaster in our office for his creative work with visuals, and gratitude to my brother-in-law, Michael Kremer, for his discriminating advice in preparation of this book so soon after his help with the last one. The shortcomings in this book, however, are solely my responsibility and, in mitigation, I can only plead they may be due to haste in pursuit of such an engaging venture.

R. Meredith Belbin

The colours of Workset ————

Colour has been much used as a form of coding and its impact is much strengthened by its emotional associations. Yet while these associations often have a common significance, they will still vary with individuals according to experience. The colours chosen for Workset have been designed to fit expectations, but where this is not possible in all cases new associations will need to be formed.

Blue is the colour most commonly associated with tradition. Here it stands for the way in which tasks have been set up in the past where instructions are passed down from a person at a higher level of authority. Blue therefore relates to structured work where the method of carrying it out is not open to question.

Yellow has been chosen with reference to the letter Y. The stem of this letter extends to two branches, implying the need for a decision at a point where two paths diverge. Yellow covers personal responsibility where the individual is held accountable for the outcome.

Green is the colour of the environment and of nature. It is a colour to which we must respond with sensitivity. Green tasks are unstructured and call for the individual to respond appropriately to them as they arise.

Orange is the colour of a round fruit, and conveys the shape of the table around which sit people of equal rank. Orange has been chosen as the colour of shared decision making.

Grey is a somewhat indefinite colour having no clear affinity to any of the preceding core colours. It is marked by the Jobholder where it is peripheral to the work assigned without being either of an innovative or of a wasted character.

White Work is the colour of a blank sheet of paper and of virgin snow. There is no mark upon it so that anything that appears on its surface must by its nature be new. White Work therefore signifies innovation.

Pink Work is the colour of fantasy, of pink elephants and pink panthers. We call it work and it may be time consuming; but it is work only in the imagination, for in reality it accomplishes nothing.

Every discrete form of work therefore can be classified according to the way in which it is perceived by the Jobholder or intended by the manager.

1

Orders and disorders ─────────

A manager is a person who assigns work to others. The art of assigning work is therefore central to the business of management even though in the past it has scarcely been recognized as an art and has been conceived mainly in contractual terms. The manager specifies requirements and, in return for a willingness to comply, the worker receives a wage. That is the lynchpin of the relationship between manager and the worker. Any failure to heed a work instruction, on the one hand, or to pay the agreed wage, on the other, means that the contract collapses.

It has therefore become prudent for anyone wishing for work to carry out an instruction exactly according to the letter even if that instruction defies common sense. That position holds for minor operations and equally for major works. Take the case of a builder tendering for a contract. The architect may have despatched plans and specifications containing features which to someone with on-the-job experience leave much to be desired, given the need for a sound, speedy and efficient construction. But the builder needs to secure the business. Complaints may be expressed privately, if volubly, to a confidant. However, nothing will be said publicly for fear that the deal might collapse, so that in the event what has been specified will proceed exactly as planned. The workers on the site may in turn complain, as they often do, that all the materials are not arriving on schedule, unaware that a specified component is difficult to obtain from a supplier and that the architect is not prepared to accept substitutes. Grumbling may rumble through the site, especially if the shortage affects their bonus payments. But its consequences will be limited. On planning issues the building workers will usually avoid confrontation or any open challenge to management's prerogative to manage, because they too need the assurance of continued work.

Such is the arrangement of pressures that in the normal course of events all orders are there to be accepted. 'It's more than my job's worth ...', says the respondent, if invited by a third party to do anything out of line. This can even be an understatement of the real dilemma given the fact that at one end of this imperative scale lies the military command. Here compliance is more than a matter of discretion and convention. During the First World War soldiers who ran away, fearing for their lives during artillery bombardments, were court-martialled and shot. It was virtually safer for apprehensive soldiers to stay put even at the risk of being little more than cannon-fodder.

Less pressing than a military command is an instruction. Instructions are the form in which orders are transmitted to employees. While they do not carry the same force as commands, they need to be heeded, for failure to do so could result in reduced promotion prospects or even in the loss of a job. At the most indulgent end of this spectrum is the type of instruction issued not as between people but in conjunction with a consumer product. That instruction comes impersonally in a manual or leaflet. The decision to read the instruction, or not to do so, is a voluntary matter and may be of little more than incidental concern to the manufacturer. Some starting instructions, for example, are buried in bulky manuals that cover several varieties of a product, including ones not being purchased, and are in several languages. To hunt through the manual in order to find the appropriate passage can be quite demanding. But to ignore an instruction will increase the chances of an unhappy experience in the use of the product or may even invite peril. Even so, it is hardly to be expected that a dissatisfied customer would bother to write to a manufacturer with suggestions on improving the instruction manual.

These varieties of command and instruction, while different in form and urgency, have two common features. The first is the need to attend to what is being imparted if unfortunate consequences are not to ensue. The second is that the receiver is passively placed at the end of a system primarily designed for downwards communication.

The causes of disorder

All recurring disorders can be viewed as some form of cybernetic failure. No system can function well if there is no means of receiving self-regulating feedback that can modify the intensity or nature of the input. That principle holds equally for all advanced systems, whether they are electrical, electromechanical or biological. Yet in the field of human affairs sight is easily lost of this basic design point, for people are inclined to believe that the human capacity for speech can always compensate. Were this so, the question must be posed as to why the receiver of a command or instruction cannot easily rectify the situation whenever trouble is encountered. The answer, in most instances, is that there is an absence of any socially sanctioned feedback loop.

In theory, of course, the problem does not sound very striking. There is no obstacle to closing the information gap, given a culture that valued openness. Ideally, the builder would be able to say to the architect: 'This is an unnecessarily expensive way of achieving your purpose. We have had good experience with an alternative material which is easier to handle and stands up to the conditions better.' For his part, the building worker would say to the master builder: 'We spend a lot of time waiting around for supplies. You are not always in touch with what is going on. Why don't you supply us with a mobile phone and let us order the materials ourselves from the builder's merchant? Then we can be sure they will arrive when we are ready.'

These responses sound reasonable enough. But, in practice, there is little chance that they would be accepted, for besides the risk of being seen as impertinences they infringe the principle of individual responsibility. The architect is held responsible for specifying how the building is to be constructed and the master builder is responsible for bringing together the men and the materials. Someone would soon retort: 'If we were to carry on in the way proposed, goodness knows what might happen. We would not know who was responsible for what.' Inevitably a further objection would be to raise the question of the competence and qualifications of the persons suggesting an extension of their personal responsibilities.

It is clear that the attempt to introduce an element of common sense or ambition into organization soon runs up against barriers. The persistent disorders of a simple, easily understood, mode of management organization are preferred to a more socially intricate system that might function better.

The current system, whatever its shortcomings, has the merit of being easy to follow. Managers, being responsible people, are given responsibility. Workers, being of lesser standing, are given tasks. That is why it is important to know who is the boss round here. When the boss is away, the system is inclined to break down and misfortune is apt to strike. Necessary activities are neglected. No-one is prepared to take decisions. People stand around waiting. Then the boss will be heard to complain: 'It is difficult to find anyone in this firm who will take responsibility.'

We are now facing a circular argument. People who are not made responsible shirk responsibilities and therefore never become responsible. And the fewer the people who take responsibilities, the greater the burden of responsibility that falls on a single person's shoulders. The phenomena of the problem and the causes of the problem become one and the same.

The essence of the crisis is that, while the management model is simple, people are complicated. Those in responsible jobs can disappoint and those in subordinate roles can surprise others by their initiative and enterprise. Here there is no rule of thumb that gives the clue. When people do not fit the managerial paradigm within which they are meant to operate, anomalies give rise to disorder and set in motion a second round of derivative anomalies as people attempt to find their way around a problem. To the discerning there is only one solution – to utilize the informal system in preference to the formal system while at the same time treating the formal system with all the due respect that it does not deserve.

The gap between the offical and unofficial systems opens the way for political operators to seize the opportunity and exercise their unwelcome skills. Once the straightforward management model of division between managers and workers fails to correspond adequately with the reality, others learn to manipulate the system, undermining authority without adding value.

An overswing of the pendulum

If the problem of issuing orders in accordance with a hierarchical formula produces a chain reaction of complications, a general reluctance to issue orders can soon become the favoured position. Throughout history one extreme has given rise to its opposite. Overindulgence in liquor produced Prohibition in the USA. Fasting follows feasting. The social extravaganza stimulates the retreat. So it is with orders. In a society in which equality is held on a pedestal, surpassing even liberty and fraternity, it is entirely predictable that an influential school of thought would arise in which it would be considered incorrect to order anyone to do anything.

I have come across several instances of this in the domestic households of busy professional women. Someone whose energies are directed at improving communications and teamwork in a large organization, and which often creates a whole set of associated values, may also need to run a household. That often leads to the employment of a domestic helper, often on a part-time basis. Such a helper may engage in the work in which the self would engage if sufficient time were available. The 'other self' may do the shopping, collect the children from school and run the household generally, in which connection the self will identify with the 'other self'. One person will do what the other is unable to do. In consequence the relationship is likely to be close and cordial.

But suppose the professional woman has a full-time job, or, in the event of having a part-time job, declines to undertake certain household tasks? Now a different condition arises. The duties of the domestic helper will need to be set out more formally. And since the self will no longer be in a position to attend to whatever work is left undone, it is important to ensure by some means or other that the duties are carried out in the way that is laid down. Now suppose the professional woman, instead of issuing instructions and departing for work as usual, has a free day at home. Not uncommonly, a new and troubling situation arises, for the full-time helper may not behave in the same way as the 'other self' and prefer to take her meals and other refreshments separately. This unexpected reaction can often create a sense of shock for a professional woman brought up in the egalitarian values prevailing in a professional working environment or influenced by the culture of firms where, typically, several eating areas or canteens may have been consolidated into a single dining area which all are expected to use. Naturally, our professional woman feels the same practice should apply at home if she is to remain true to her values. However, the reality is that the decision of what to eat together and where to eat it is capable of producing a mutual sense of embarrassment. The result is that either the one or the other announces she does not feel hungry and the shared meal fails to take place.

A problem here is that we have not fully developed a new mode of working relationship but neither have we escaped the pull of the traditional system. Giving and receiving orders involves a status difference and typically generates social distance. If, however, the provider of work wishes to remove social distance and to establish a closer personal relationship, a set of associated behavioural modifications has to be introduced. Forms of address become more intimate, Christian names replace titles and orders become requests.

However, the price to be paid for this change in approach is that tasks cannot be given and supervised to the same extent. While servants in the Victorian era worked to exacting standards, being subject to a domineering regime, their counterparts in the modern era are very differently placed. They expect to negotiate crucial aspects of their employment and agreement should not be presumed. Tasks still retain their menial character and the dilemma for the manager is to make the nature of the work sound and feel worthy and acceptable without dropping standards. It is a dilemma that most managers do not handle very well. The way in which work is set up and distributed here represents a major problem.

Person images and task images

When work is considered as falling into only two types, that involving responsibility which is discharged by the bosses and that involving tasks specified by bosses but carried out by workers, it becomes inevitable that involvement in a lower grade of work has considerable repercussions. First, it can damage a person's social standing in a hierarchy. Second, on a wider front, it impinges directly on the rate and nature of industrial development. In Third World countries, especially, technical graduates are notoriously unwilling to embroil themselves in practical shopfloor matters, preferring to sit in their offices as befits those who aspire to be proper executives. It is all a matter of status. That is one of the primary reasons, so it has been alleged, why multinationals in process industries are reluctant to locate substantial manufacturing establishments in underdeveloped parts of the world that cry out for investment.

In the developed world the distinction in the distribution of the two types of work is less marked. The blurring begins at the level of the household. The availability of so much labour-saving equipment means that many domestic tasks have been taken over by machines. The remaining domestic chores can be shared. In a professional household where both husband and wife are working the division of domestic labour is a matter for negotiation. Aptitudes, individual preferences and personal availability at particular times of the day all play their part. These are essentially private matters which are not readily visible to third parties nor consequentially transferable to the outside world.

For my part, my practical skills in the household are generally limited. But, happily, I can claim a certain distinction in two areas – the ability to stop babies crying and a capacity for peeling potatoes. With regard to the latter, which has the greater utility in the domestic scene, I take a potato peeler, which is right-handed in preference to one designed for left-handers, and clasping it in the left hand push it in rapid movements away from the body, whereas others draw the potato peeler towards the body. In a potato-peeling competition I would be likely to outpeel most housewives. It is a skill I hoped would come in handy when resident with a family during extended overseas engagements. There are occasions when I have felt especially grateful to the wife of a fellow professional on finding that, without any prompting, some of my clothing has been removed from my bedroom to be later returned washed, ironed and neatly folded. In return, I am keen to peel the potatoes. But my offers have always been graciously refused, often with a smile, as though I was making an absurd suggestion. It does seem that my general image does not fit that particular task.

The willingness of people to take on a range of work is growing not only by couples sharing in households but also by employees in firms. In many occupations versatility in dealing with varying demands and situations is more highly valued than superproductivity in some given activity. That is the way in which industry has been moving and its implications are profound. It means that the carrying out of relatively simple tasks and the discharge of important responsibilities have become intertwined. The social revolution at work means that the executive who would previously dictate letters to a secretary now sits in front of a word processor and for a time resembles a worker in the typing pool. Directors now act as their own chauffeurs. No longer is it counted extraordinary for a director to break a journey to deliver an urgently needed parcel in the course of driving to a meeting with a customer.

In these instances tasks which would have been performed as a result of orders are being undertaken voluntarily. But the image problem remains a possible impediment, for whether tasks are acceptable or not for persons of a certain status level remains questionable. Clearly, the image needs to be brought into line with the reality. Work cannot be organized, covertly, on the basis that tasks might be undertaken voluntarily by someone holding important responsibilities. On the other hand, there would be a reluctance to include such tasks in a person's job description for fear of creating an insult, for tasks are activities that are ladled out to those of lower rank.

This is the essence of the unresolved crisis that lies at the heart of current work organization. Should traditional ways of dividing up work, often of proven value, be retained or not? And if that pattern is found wanting, what is the next step? How otherwise should work be grouped, distributed and communicated to those who are to undertake it?

The time has at last arrived in the evolution of the world of work when the questions become worth posing. Yet when I have asked them, I have met only a stunned silence.

2

The true nature of a modern job ——————

The issue of how a job should be set up has far-reaching consequences for both the vitality of businesses and its impact on society. Yet on the whole it is not a matter that is widely recognized; nor has it excited much attention among managers themselves, since the general presumption in hierarchical organizations is that the position is basically simple. When a job has to be done, the person in charge should make it clear exactly what work has to be performed, demonstrate if necessary how it is to be done and routinely check that the orders, or instructions, have been followed. Such an outlook inevitably lends itself to a systematic approach of which the most advanced was termed Scientific Management, otherwise eponymously known as Taylorism.

Taylor believed that, where work was concerned, there was one best way of doing anything. Once waste was cut out by studying the most efficient way of performing a job, the ideal method could then be introduced as standard to bring about recurring benefits. It was a short step to encourage a worker to perform in the desired way by providing closely supervised training followed by bonus payments relating to the output achieved against the expected yardstick of performance. Scientific Management led not only to greater efficiency but also to the prospects that productive workers could share in the rising standard of living.

That spirit gave the clue to the very essence of a modern job in the period immediately following the Second World War. It was Taylored to the age, in more senses than one. Productivity was all. Since long years of enforced austerity had resulted in great shortages, manufacturing now occupied the key ground in business. Sales was indistinguishable from distribution. There was an expectation of infinite demand for whatever was produced.

My personal introduction to this burgeoning post-war concept of a modern job had come about by being plunged into my first appointment after leaving my alma mater, the University of Cambridge. My doctoral dissertation had taken me into industry, now to become for me an everlasting source of fascination. As soon as my academic work had finished I was invited to apply for a research fellowship at Cranfield. As it happened, the field was one that did not interest me at all, for the topic was an investigation into compensating rest allowances. What that meant was that highly efficient workers performing jobs in the ideal manner could be expected to have rest breaks to enable them to recover from work fatigue. The question was what sort of work justified what sort of fatigue allowance. Scientific managers expected a scientific answer to that question too.

The reason I accepted the appointment was that Cranfield had established a name for itself as being one of the academic institutions most closely involved with the realities of industrial work. When I arrived to inspect the establishment I was impressed by the unquenchable enthusiasm of the professor, Jim Connolly, who had inaugurated the first work study school in a college. There he set up a demonstration department comprising workplace jobs shown both before and after the application of work study. Huge productivity increases could be shown. A constant stream of industrial visitors poured through the department to marvel at these accomplishments. Naturally, senior managers were keen to send their people on courses so that they could be taught how to reap the benefits of this new approach. And so Cranfield became the number one spot for work study in the United Kingdom.

I joined the Department of Economics and Production, as it was then called, shortly after the work study school was founded within it. Decades later this emergent body was transformed into the Cranfield Management School, and became so large that if a visitor were to inquire casually about the size of its academic staff I doubt that any one person would come up with the same precise number. By contrast, its forerunner, during much of the period when it made its name, comprised a staff of merely two active members.

Barney Carver was the time and motion man from Hoovers. With a short crisp moustache, an efficient delivery and a sense of humour so dry that to laugh would have been out of place, he had acquired a deserved reputation for setting rates for the job and bonus payments that could seldom be faulted. His colleague, Lance Harper, was a tall, sandy-haired, inspired and flamboyant figure with a glamorous wife and a capacity for reeling off seemingly endless verses of the bawdy song 'Eskimo Nell' at the termination of final course parties. At the start of each course he would open his lectures on method study with the question: is the job always necessary? The answer, illustrated with striking examples and lateral-thinking solutions, was to be 'no'. The message was that only when the necessity of the job had been established should time and motion begin.

This seemingly incongruous pair combined especially well. But the workload was heavy, so soon I was drafted in, even though a relative junior at the time, to become a third lecturing member, and conferring on the school, it was hoped, a respectable academic balance. My brief was to cover ergonomics, the scientific study of work. My credentials rested on having joined the Ergonomics Research Society shortly after its foundation and having undertaken short engagements to launch the subject in Holland and Italy.

Visiting lecturers to the school included Annie Shaw, the founder of the Ann Shaw Organization. Annie was a close personal friend of Lillian Gilbreth, from whose name in reverse, therbligs, became the stock in trade for describing units of work among motion study experts; but in the wider world she was better known for using her managerial skills in her large family through her famed book *Cheaper by the Dozen*. In these pioneering days it was easy to believe that with method, motion and time study the theory of a modern job had reached its zenith.

The work study school lacked a formal head. To the dismay of the duo in charge, an elder statesman of impeccable industrial pedigree and suitable gravitas was brought in to fill the position. He obliged by dying soon after appointment and the school then continued during the consequent interregnum happily as before. At the suggestion of Ann Shaw the next appointee was Seymour Hills, a man with the distinction of having stood against Winston Churchill in a parliamentary election. He expired in a motor accident in which no other vehicle was involved. So the work study school resumed as a headless organization, steadily increasing its reputation throughout the period. Such a state of affairs cannot continue indefinitely, nor did it, since any visiting Mr Big naturally expects to meet his counterpart. It is all an inevitable matter of expectations built around the way in which society is structured. Nevertheless, the experience served as a transient object lesson in how well an institution can run without a boss and was the first of several such examples I have encountered throughout my working life.

The decline of the operator

The momentum of the scientific study of the worker continued. On the other side of the Atlantic the term 'work study' would have been unfamiliar, for there existed an equivalent term, 'human engineering'. The very make-up of this word suggested a branch of the mechanical sciences with people being seen primarily as limbs rather than minds. At least it was to the credit of ergonomics that the subject increasingly focused on the interface between man and machine in an attempt to use the best features that each could bring to a man–machine system. The consequence of this examination turns out to be that machines have the better limbs and people have the better minds. The only exception in the latter case is where the regularities of thought processes permit computer programming.

The next advance in scientific study of the job promised to open up a whole new era but eventually turned out to lead into an eventual blind alley. Time study had involved standing over a worker with a stopwatch, an activity that was labour-intensive and sometimes politically contentious. The new alternative, predetermined motion times, seemed a softer option, for it could be contained in a book and used like a ready reckoner. Provided the workers' movements could be analysed into their constituent therbligs, or basic elements, the time for a job could be calculated without the rate fixer ever leaving the desk or even before the job came into being. This far-reaching approach soon found application in assembly operations, especially those involving small parts and necessitating fine movements. Several competing systems of predetermined motions times arose, of which the best known was MTM.

The whole of these foregoing activities was encompassed by the term 'work measurement'. Whether by stopwatch or by the compilation of synthetic figures, a time could be prepared for the job. All that had to be presumed for the economic justification of this approach was that the situation would remain stable. Therein lay the fallacy.

Two forces now started to operate independently to undermine all this painstaking development. Predictable and repetitive work now became susceptible to a radical solution from another quarter – the special-purpose machine. Hence the work of the routine operator fell away in importance. Increasingly the machine did the physical work and the emphasis shifted away from muscles and dexterity to the employment of a new breed of workers with knowledge and skill and problem-solving abilities, workers who could liaise with others and cope with contingencies. It was a trend conspicuous not only in the UK but also in countries throughout the world. New investment shifted to the sophisticated areas of developed countries and cheap unskilled or semi-skilled labour no longer had the same economic attractions of a former era.

The second force to exert its effects arose from a progressive but ultimately massive change in market conditions. As shortages were overcome, producers lost their dominant hold. Henry Ford could once say: 'You can have any colour you like provided it's black'. But now the message was that any colour and any preferred style had to be met. The early formula had been 'make it, then sell it'. Now, increasingly, manufacturers would not make it until they were sure it would sell. No operation could be set up with confidence that it would run and run.

The philosophy of Scientific Management, once the rage, was eroded by the growing discontinuities now characterizing the workplace. Stripped of its modern image it disappeared at remarkable speed. It was an object lesson in Oscar Wilde's famous comment: 'Fashion is so quickly dated'. Management fashions come and go with equal alacrity and leave behind them a wardrobe of unused clothes.

Not modern enough

With the sophisticated techniques of work measurement becoming less applicable to the conditions of modern industry some alternative stance was called for. After leaving Cranfield, which had been at the cutting edge of the more exact approach, I was to encounter the full range of simpler ways of setting up the job. The various options could be described as occupying different points along a continuuum.

The most closely defined jobs were covered by a Job Specification. Here the contents of the work are precisely set out, though less fully than as a result of work measurement. A Job Description is one grade further down the line with an approach to its subject couched in more general terms. Finally, at the far end of the scale stood the least defined where the comment is sometimes made 'throw them in at the deep end and they will sort themselves out'. Here there is no written paperwork at all to guide the worker on what to do and what not to do.

Somewhere down the line one of these, it might be thought, had to be right. In the event, all three ran into difficulties, of which the issues surrounding the Job Specification became the most serious.

The idea of the Job Specification was commended by the same seeming logic that underlay Taylorism. If everbody knows exactly what they have to do and they do it, we should have the perfect formula for efficiency. An influx of management consultants was soon to invade industry engaged in setting up combined programmes of Job Specification and Job Evaluation, with which it was usually twinned. The whole strategy rested on taking a particular view of a job.

For a time all was well. But the ramifications of this introduction had clearly not been foreseen. It was not long before managers, or co-workers, were requesting employees to engage in activities not covered by their Job Specification. That document, now being treated as a personal contract, was to prove a hindrance to progress, for either the desired cooperation was lacking ('That's not my job') or, if the work was undertaken, a claim would be made for increased pay on the grounds of additional responsibilities. In the public sector pay awards were subject to the closest scrutiny and often could not be given. So the situation arose of prospective deadlock – no extra pay so no extra work. However, there was a way round the problem. Instead of paying the workers more, more workers could be taken on at the rate for the job formally judged correct according to Job Evaluation. That process is said to have accounted for the connection between the introduction of Job Specification in the various departments of local authorities and the sudden rise in the number of their employees. To sum up, Job Specifications led in practice either to wage inflation or overmanning, and sometimes to both.

Job Descriptions are scaled-down versions of Job Specifications. Their greater vagueness is an advantage in one sense since infringements of the contract are less evident and do not become contentious sticking points. But in another sense they create some problems. While they imply a definite work territory, the boundaries of that territory are not sufficiently clear-cut to avert disputes on the interpretation of duties between neighbouring workers. Since the Job Description is tailored for the individual, it cannot readily serve the function of dealing with the duties and activities of the dynamic group.

The question I now posed to myself is: what happens if there is no Job Specification and no Job Description; what happens when there is nothing? Here there was no need to speculate. Most small firms I found to be in exactly that position. Their systems were informal and in any case they lacked the facilities for the requisite administration. Further, there were a few medium-sized and larger firms that deliberately avoided Job Specifications and Job Descriptions as alien to their basic philosophy.

Small firms got round the problem because its members knew one another intimately and operated as in a family. They did what is needed which is why they went without job titles. Should anyone act out of line there was always the paterfamilias to exercise authority.

Some larger firms at the present day have adopted a similar approach but against a different background. The movement against Job Titles, Job Specifications and Job Descriptions is bound up with the move against Departmentalism. Formalism is being discarded as a means of generating business dynamics. Some companies have been transformed through being 're-engineered'. Groups of people have taken responsibility for the conduct, control and profitability of particular businesses. The view is that these need to be managed in a holistic way. There can be no passing of the buck. There is no opportunity to say 'This is your job, this is mine'. Teamwork has replaced individualism.

Teamwork does not, of course, guarantee in itself good results. As in sport, there can be good teams and poor teams. And, as in sport, it all depends on how the players play together. Here the conduct of 're-engineered' businesses can find itself on shaky ground. There are initial savings to be made by re-engineering because the general clutter in procedures in the accumulation of people becomes exposed as soon as a business is stripped to its core. All that is surplus to requirements can be disposed of and a new dynamism created. But the new leanness depends on getting everything right. With middle management removed and the formalities of job responsibilities taken away, the demanaged and dejobbed surviving body is prone to what has been called corporate anorexia. The ultimate price of slimming is lack of energy for any new advance.

There is a cure, of sorts, for this ailment which I witnessed in a number of cases. The reaction was a return to something closer to the former system. A new strong man was appointed while a part of the new culture would be retained. In effect, a synthesis of hybrid character emerged. Was this going to be the forerunner of a growing trend? I asked myself.

The instabilities of the new system arose in the first place because the focus on removing the old was not matched by a comparable amount of attention on what the new required. The decision-making powers of middle managers need to be redistributed. But to whom? Surely not to everyone equally? That would remove the division of labour and function that is the essence of economic strength. Managing the distribution of tasks and responsibilities is the key to getting things right in the first place. That is why any attempt to decry the role of management, as occurs in some avant-garde circles, is only likely to generate a new crisis.

The way forward must be both to manage the process and to negotiate its operation. That demands some means of classifying the work that will be commonly understood, rational in nature and acceptable to the people concerned. Formerly nearly every job was clear-cut in terms of its trade skills and its boundaries of operation. But the essence of a modern job is that it consists in the words of one jobholder of 'a bit of this, a bit of that and a bit of the other'. Tasks and responsibilities intermingle, as does individual work and group work. Job boundaries have become so indistinct that the very word 'job' is being questioned in some quarters.

That position is understandable in the case of executives in high-tech companies. But its significance is reinforced by what is happening at lower skill levels. Even here the heterogeneity of work encompassed within a job is growing. Consider the position with van drivers in some small and medium-sized firms. In some cases 'outsourcing' has taken over their jobs and the full-time van driver is under threat. Such a worker can complain 'No, the job is not being lost but I am losing the job'. But some other van drivers are observed to enjoy greater security in their employment: characteristically they fulfil a greater range of activities within the firm. When van driving is not needed they engage in a spot of labouring and cleaning and packing; and though their duties in despatching may finish, they are too useful to be despatched themselves by dismissal from employment.

The modern worker needs to be versatile and yet be able to recognize the boundaries of personal work. Equally the manager needs to understand and discover what work is appropriate to the jobholder. It is a two-way process. Mutual expectations need to be built up. And it needs a method to enable it to happen.

3

Reclassifying work: tasks versus responsibilities ————

The modern job offers increasing opportunity for discretion as choices need to be made on how time is spent on various tasks and responsibilities; on whether work is conducted privately or in the company of others. The fact that responsibilities have been added to the tasks workers have been traditionally set elevates the status of the worker. Correspondingly, it lessens the distinction between workers and 'executives'.

That is why a general language based on the composition of tasks and responsibilities is a good way of looking at the modern job for all who are engaged in work. Yet to approach the subject in this way runs inevitably into the difficulty of how best to create a common understanding. That much I realized on the very first occasion as I was introducing the subject of tasks and responsibilities to a management group when one of the participants took issue with me about my use of words. 'The tasks we set people these days involve responsibility and only responsible people can carry them out satisfactorily' he claimed. The implication was that the division between tasks and responsibility was a wholly artificial one.

The objection seemed reasoned and was not easy to refute without a pause for thought. Here I felt I was up against a formidable problem I had encountered before. The difficulty is that meaning in language is largely context-bound. Many common words, whose meaning we take for granted, are used in a variety of ways, as reference to any larger dictionary will show. To add to this difficulty, such words can carry personal associations which can evoke a particular set of emotive reactions. And then there is indiscipline in the use of words. Many problems are caused by the Humpty Dumptys of this world – 'When *I* use a word, it means what I choose it to mean'. It is small wonder that much debate revolves round words and easily diverts attention from matters of substance.

Yet I was not deflected, for I could see an important issue lay lurking that had long been obscured. In spite of the obstacle of language and of the various interpretations to which it can give rise, I reached the view that, in principle, tasks and responsibilities were mutually exclusive. A person who is set a task by a manager and agrees to undertake it cannot be held responsible for the outcome. In the event of failure it is perfectly fair to state 'Well, that's what you told me to do'. Conversely, a person who carries responsibility for an outcome cannot legitimately be given orders on how to proceed. Such a person can always argue: 'Well, it's my job to decide'.

Blue and Yellow Work: individual operations

To press home the operational advantages of using mutually exclusive terms for the purposes of work organization, some device would be needed to free us from the tyranny of words. Here it occurred to me that the distinction in the demands of work could be better handled by the use of colour sets. One colour can designate one thing and a second colour another. Except among the colour-blind, two colours cannot be confused nor will the meanings attached to them. The colours are, of course, co-terminous with words but soon the colours become the dominant means of communication. Particular tasks carried out in a particular way and assigned to an individual I decided could be denoted as Blue Work. Here the choice of blue was made on grounds of its association with tradition. That is, classical Blue Work comes from orders received from a boss as in a command structure.

The contrast here is with Yellow Work, where an individual is charged with responsibility for an outcome and is judged by how well that outcome is achieved. Yellow was the colour selected since its first letter comprises a stem with two arms. The arms serve as a symbolic choice point, for the essence of responsibility is that it involves choices and decisions.

In practice, a jobholder may be presented with a combination of Blue Work and Yellow Work, in which case it is important in any assessment of performance that the two should be treated on a separate plane. A person may not be equally good at both. Further, interest in the two fields may diverge so that a person will focus on the one at the expense of the other. These were more than suppositions, for they corresponded with what I had commonly observed in practice. Brilliant performance and neglect often travel hand in hand. But few would find it worth while to embark on any interventionist action if the jobholder had made a mark on the main part of the job.

Green and Orange Work: shared operations

The next area of work to be charted out involved a shift in focus from individual to group work. Here again it is essential to underline the differences between tasks and responsibilities.

Shared tasks are those constructed by a social process even if the tasks themselves are ultimately conducted individually. Here the task-work carried out depends to some degree on the social environment, since people differ in what they want and what they expect, depending on the situation and the personalities involved. Unlike Blue Work, the tasks in which people engage have no firmly set and sharp features. Instead, their environmentally affected nature suggests the appropriateness of the colour green. Green Work therefore refers to tasks which are given their final shape by the way in which people communicate with one another in particular situations. Wherever people need discussion immediately before they start to do something, Green Work figures. Green Work also covers tasks that can be split up between two or more people and when tackled in this way makes the work easier, as in making beds or moving furniture even without the necessity of oral communication. Another variant of Green Work involves an initiator and a responder. The initiator identifies an immediate problem, the responder suggests how it might be tackled and together they combine to get the work done. Many services that are supplied, or can be made available by negotiation, follow that path.

Shared responsibilities differ from shared tasks in that the former entails collective accountability for whatever decisions are reached and whatever resulting actions are taken. Collective responsibility, in contrast to the personal responsibility of a single manager or boss, attaches itself to a team of people with equal or near-equal status. A round table, the likely centrepiece for their deliberations, is suggestive of the legendary table made famous by King Arthur and his knights. A round table physically resembles the letter O. So the type of work that this signifies is represented by orange as regards both the shape and particular colour of the fruit.

Effective teamwork in meeting wide-ranging responsibilities is the hallmark of a civilized society. Not all group work, however, should necessarily be equated with Orange Work, for many social groups do not behave as though at an orderly conference: there is often a lack of order and often not much evidence of work. Here I have been made aware of what is at stake by experiences in three fields of group activity.

During two previous decades, but less so in recent years, there had been a vogue in setting up communes. These were self-organizing bodies that determined their own life styles and whose members contributed to the work and income of the group in a way that

THE WORKSET CYCLE
Adding Colour and Clarity to Jobs

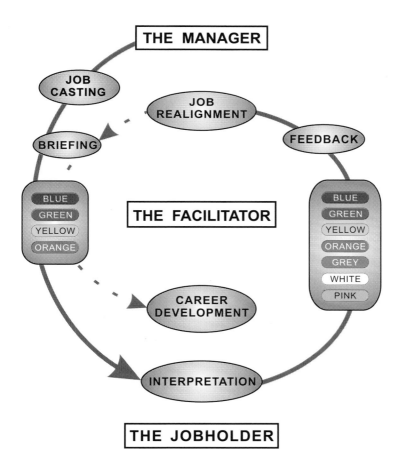

THE PROCESS APPROACH TO JOB CASTING

Plate 1

THE JOB AS VIEWED FROM TWO POSITIONS

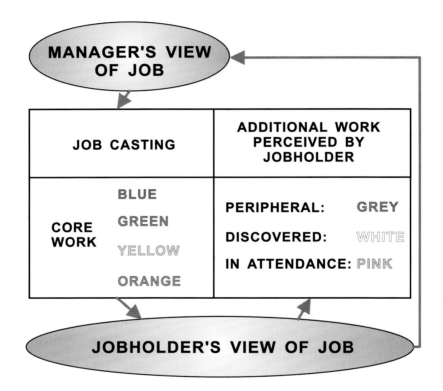

MANAGERS AND JOBHOLDERS TAKE DIFFERENT VIEWS OF A JOB. A GOOD FEEDBACK SYSTEM BRINGS BOTH VIEWS TOGETHER. *GREY* AND *WHITE* WORK CAN THEN BE INCORPORATED INTO A RECAST JOB AND STEPS TAKEN TO **MINIMIZE** *PINK*.

Plate 2

THE DYNAMIC NATURE OF A JOB

**WHITE WORK
CARRIES THE
JOB FORWARD**

WHITE

**CORE
WORK**

BLUE

YELLOW

GREEN

ORANGE

**GREY (or INCIDENTAL)
WORK, HELPS
CREATE
RESPONSIVENESS**

GREY

**PINK WORK
DRAGS THE
JOB BACK**

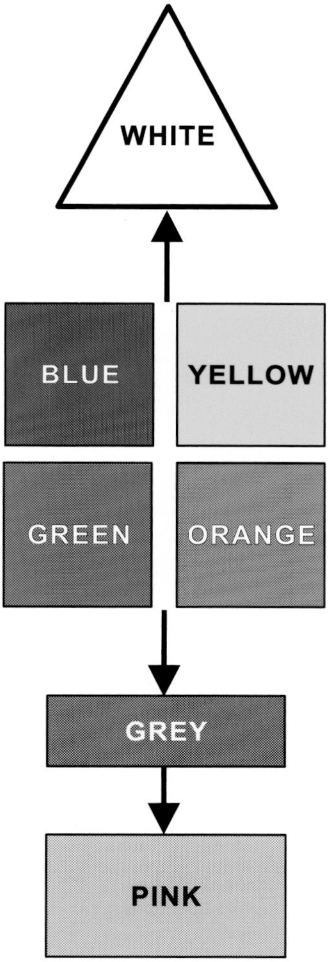

PINK

Plate 3

PROMPTING QUESTIONS FOR DIVIDING THE WORK INTO SETS

	CORE ISSUES	**FURTHER CONSIDERATIONS**
BLUE WORK	Is there a defined standard? Is there a correct way of working?	How is the standard set? Has the Jobholder been trained? Or, failing that, is subject to the necessary degree of supervision?
GREEN WORK	Does the quality of the work largely depend on how well people communicate with and relate to one another?	Does the Jobholder work well with others? Respond to needs in a flexible way?
YELLOW WORK	Can responsibility be assigned to a particular person? Is there latitude in terms of how that responsibility is discharged?	Does the Jobholder show a readiness to take responsibility? Are there criteria for assessing personal accountability?
ORANGE WORK	Does part of the work lend itself to collective responsibility? Are suitable people available	Have the necessary conditions been created for team empowerment?

Plate 4

reconciled personal freedom with group consultation. Both responsibilities and tasks are shared. The cases of which I had intimate knowledge, though only as an outsider, appear to have followed a similar path. They would begin well with their members fired up with a certain idealism. After a while the need to complete certain tasks and duties would create inevitable pressures. Some members would respond positively. Others would find the pressures incompatible with their desire for personal freedom and their concept of self-identity. The result was that work would be undertaken unevenly with the burden falling on a few. Quiet resentment would finally erupt into open complaint. The resulting quarrels would not be satisfactorily resolved, for in a non-hierarchical organization there is no ultimate arbiter to settle disputes.

Another form of statusless group working is to be found in management centres which specialize in outdoor exercises and projects. Here the aim is to learn about group processes, to discover the sense of togetherness and to gain new insights about the self in a relaxing and neutral setting. As an objective in itself that is fine. But behaviour in these exercises can also be looked at from another angle. One can consider effectiveness in undertaking a group activity. Because there is no status and no structure, individuals find difficulty in establishing any personal role. Suggestions made by one person are ignored by others. Individuals engage in activities that have not been sanctioned by the group. Others stand around and do nothing. The failure to act effectively can be shrugged off since the experience has a different intended purpose; but for some it becomes a source of concern because it raises questions to which there are no evident answers. However, these problems associated with groups have been skilfully used by some training organizations in order to launch an understanding of true teamwork.

My third example of unregulated group work relates to juries. A jury is a collection of random people who have never met before and are assembled for a single undertaking. There is no mutual knowledge, respect or understanding at the outset. Under such conditions it is a long time before any progress can be made. It is what I found myself on such occasions, and others, who have spoken of their experience in juries, have reached the same conclusion. Juries seem unable to use time effectively even though ultimately they may be effective in terms of the decisions they reach.

Group working may be a necessity for one reason or another. But to widen its application without taking steps to turn the group into a team would be a formula for stagnation. The shared acceptance and discharge of responsibilities demands a team approach. Orange Work establishes the conditions for team empowerment. Orange Work, if properly set up, turns an amorphous group into a team where each member will find a contributory role to play in meeting a common objective.

Orange Work need not necessarily indicate that numbers of people are needed before responsibility is shared, nor does it press the claim for large committees. The number who engage in Orange Work can be as small as two, especially in cases where professionals in different fields believe that a balanced judgement can be reached only if they agree. That type of small-scale consensus has to be distinguished from another that is similar in outward appearances, where a person takes evidence from a second person but reserves the right to make the final decision. Such an approach is more suggestive of Yellow Work.

Outside core work – the grey, the white and the pink

The extent to which individuals differ in the way they carry out work supposedly identical in demands has been noted by Rosemary Stewart as being of some theoretical importance in the construction of jobs. For her, the core work is the essential work that needs to be performed regardless of who does it, while pheripheral work is the variable element which may differ according to whoever is installed in the job. The significance of that observation is that it offers a strategy for defining jobs without stifling initiative. Hence the aim should be to specify the core work while allowing adequate latitude for self-expression in the extension of the job boundaries.

The first step therefore is to classify work into chunks that are meaningful, distinctive and appropriate for persons of different temperaments and aptitudes but with the added advantage of being conceptually easy to understand. Tasks are separated from responsibilities and individual work from group work to provide four cells or sets. There are individual tasks and shared tasks, individual responsibilities and shared responsibilities. These form the core of all work. Work in each of these sets, while being inescapable, needs to be established and managed in a different way, which is why Workset is the title conferred upon the system.

But there is something beyond the core. The assigning of tasks and responsibilities in the past would have been made on the presumption that the manager can with great insight classify, forecast and comprehensively specify all that has to be undertaken. Not only is this impossible, it is undesirable. Here, I confess, my views have changed over time. In the era when I received training in the various techniques of work measurement the aim was to cover all activities, without exception, in which the worker would engage. The intention underlying work planning was to detect all unoccupied time and to ensure that every moment was productively filled.

This was an ambitious goal. But the approach had two disadvantages. In the first place an enormous burden was placed on work planners to ensure that every aspect of a person's work was spelt out and underlined. That intention was time consuming in its implications and oppressive in the atmosphere created in the eyes of those subject to such highly supervised work. A second disadvantage was that no room was left for any unplanned initiative. Much the same position can arise in the truly lean company from which all possibilities of unused time have been eliminated: it has no spare energy left to devote to enterprise. The remedy here lies in budgeting for a limited amount of overmanning which provides the scope and resources for future progress, given the proviso that the culture allows and encourages all employees to contribute to development. That is why the rate of continued innovation in Japanese companies has been so impressive. When such a spirit operates at all levels a lot of minor improvements add up to a big step ahead of the competition.

A desirable strategy, then, for setting up work is to focus on the core of what has to be done with the clear understanding that surrounding this core there will be other activities that the person in the job will see as worth doing. This peripheral work surrounding the core would not justify the time that would be needed to spell it out. Many of these activities have only marginal consequences for the outcome of the job and yet should not be neglected if the job is to run smoothly. This type of indefinite work is defined as Grey Work. It is never specified by managers but nonetheless it is always of interest to know where involvement in peripheral work is detracting from time that should be spent on core work.

A shortage of core work carries one benefit in that it creates opportunities for initiatives, although it must be conceded that not all employees will make a contribution along such lines even if given the chance. Nevertheless, an employee who makes one or two useful suggestions often has the potential to make a recurring contribution in pushing forward the frontiers of progress. For such a person the work boundaries and opportunities deserve continued attention: in the eyes of the individual it is called career development. On the other hand, the person with a totally conservative approach to work is valuable in other ways and there is no point in providing surplus time for a contribution that cannot be made.

Since it is too restricting to fill working time entirely with tasks and responsibilities, some space needs to be left for the spontaneous growth of productive ideas. That is how new plans arise that result in a rescheduling of tasks and responsibilities to form some new advance. Improvements of that nature are termed White Work. It is as though one is starting with a blank sheet with no instructions. The empty page is the only invitation to a contribution. White is chosen as being the colour of a blank page, if indeed the term colour is appropriate to white. But, more than that, it is the symbol of innocence. The person who puts forward a suggestion should don the clothes of simplicity and modesty in advance. The more radical the idea, the more sweeping the innovation, the more likely it is to arouse opposition and even anger. It may even prove a false lead, for progress can never be guaranteed.

The maxim for White Work is 'Think, study and improve'. It can apply at any level. But it will not apply to everyone, only to those to whom it is fitting because they have the capacity to use it to good effect. It might be presumed that White Work embraces all research and development. That would be a mistake, for much work in that area is highly structured and typically involves routine measurement and testing: it is largely Blue Work. White Work can only refer to the unplanned, to the spontaneously proactive, to that which lies beyond the core work of set tasks and responsibilities.

Most of the space that provides opportunities for White Work is not used to that end but is frittered away. That is not to say it is spent in idleness. It is embarrassing for any worker or executive to be seen sitting down conspicuously doing nothing. A variety of behavioural disguises are available. Unnecessary phone calls can be made. Objects can be rearranged. Conversations can be started up that have a specious connection with work but which have no useful outcome and are largely made for social reasons. The opportunities for ineffective work are endless.

While much ineffective work is entered into voluntarily, there is another type that comes about at the behest of others. People are called to meetings ostensibly designed to provide information, but in the event, largely consisting of one individual airing personal views. Those leaving the meeting exclaim inwardly, and sometimes outwardly 'What a waste of time'. Waiting is another form of activity, or rather inactivity, that can be imposed. Someone fails to turn up for a scheduled meeting. Builders on a building site hang about with little attempt to look busy, as they await delivery of materials that arrive only after a complaining telephone call.

During this period of time employees are 'in attendance'. No useful work is being done but this idleness is not the idleness of sloth. Instead, it reflects the failure of management to plan and supply an adequate flow of work. Alternatively, it can reflect that failure of the team to own responsibility for the effective use of its time, preferring to believe that responsibility rests on the shoulders of some higher authority or the elusive and distant 'them'.

'In Attendance' now becomes a Workset and the fact that no useful work is performed within it is immaterial. In the language of work measurement what was termed 'unoccupied time' became an area of opportunity for method study and hence for improved labour productivity. In Attendance incorporates unoccupied time to which must be added occupied time spent ineffectively. If work is to be reassigned to advantage, some measure of what constitutes In Attendance time needs to be set out and there is no better person to record its composition than the person in the job. The only proviso is that this should be recognized as a valid form of categorizing work activity, since it can occur in every job, and that its identification should not denote censure on the person to whom it is attached.

The significance of In Attendance in work assignment demands a colour and the choice of colour becomes an important issue. I had thought of labelling it black, as though it was some black hole into which activity that might otherwise be useful disappears. But here it was pointed out that I might be taken to task by casting ethnic aspersions or of summoning up a funereal air. If people are willing to cite unfruitful time openly, a more cheerful and inviting colour is needed. A colleague made the admirable suggestion of pink on the grounds of its association with fantasy, as with pink elephants or the Pink Panther. In Attendance therefore becomes Pink Work: a fantasy that a person at work is apparently busy, sometimes even frantically busy, without being able to point to any actual output. I confess there are occasions when my day has been dominated by Pink Work and I say to myself 'What exactly have I accomplished today?' The review of the day's proceedings fails to find any satisfactory answer and it becomes difficult to reconstruct what I have been doing and to justify the day's events.

The seven colour sets in producing unambiguous visual differentiation between classes of work replace semantic differentiation with their more indefinite boundaries of meaning. Yet because people think more in terms of words than colours, it will be helpful for many to return to words to turn an abstract representation into meaning. That will provide a mini-dictionary that is suggested takes the following form:

Blue equals structured task work
Yellow equals decision work
Green equals reactive work
Orange equals collaborative work
Grey equals peripheral work
White equals spontaneously creative work
Pink equals unproductive work

Managing the colour spectrum

The chosen sets of work have come to the fore through years of study of team roles; through looking at how individuals with given team-role profiles approach and interpret their job, in noticing how they are attracted to the demands of some work items but avoid engaging in others.

If everyone could take on exactly the work that appealed, all would be fine. But the world is not like that. Work has to be handled as it comes; and it comes in all shapes and sizes. In my previous book *Team Roles at Work* I made the point that where demands are made on a person that are out of line with the natural team-role profile it is good personal strategy to make a team-role sacrifice. In other words, a different role has to be played from that which is preferred. But that sacrifice should be temporary. Otherwise either personal strain will build up or the individual will revert suddenly to a natural form of team-role behaviour that appears incongruous and unwelcome in the given situation.

Here I failed to take account of the more usual reaction to a work demand that does not appeal to the individual. The reaction is one of avoidance. People distribute their working time in the way they think fit. This allows them to appear busy but underneath the superficial appearance the reality of the job has changed and often in a way that for a considerable time escapes the notice of management. Sometimes the significance of this interpretation of the job only comes to light when a person leaves and is replaced by another who is given the same job description. The two behaviours are then found to be very different from one another. Occasionally a person's interpretation of the job is so out of line with what is required yet masked by such a compensating display of busy activity that the true position is only revealed by a prolonged absence, as can be caused by illness. Then it comes to light that no-one misses the absentee and no extra workload has had to be passed on to others.

The nature of a modern job is that, due to the fluctuating variety of its demands, it requires continuous interpretation. It is fitting that the interpreter is the person in the job, the jobholder. But if that interpretation is at variance with the original intentions of the job as conceived by the manager, it could mean one of two things either of which are matters of some importance.

The first is that the work of the jobholder has migrated from that which was originally set out, so leaving a shortfall that in the long run is likely to cause problems. The second is that the jobholder is more in touch with what is needed than the manager. The jobholder will, in effect, have created another job within the shell of the old one. In which case should the old shell be cast off? Should the new one be recognized in its place? To these questions there is no ultimate answer until the reasons are examined for the discrepancy between the manager's forecast on the use of time and the nature of its actual deployment as recorded by the jobholder.

The seven sets of work provide a framework for examining the discrepancies, for making comparisons on how notional work differs from actual work, for creating a basis for dialogue; and, finally, for facilitating the consequential decisions that need to be reached on the best possible fit between people and jobs.

4
'So what's the job?' ───────────

A job is an assembly of given tasks and responsibilities undertaken in return for remuneration. It follows that any job applicant should be entitled to know what a prospective appointment entails. And, equally, it follows that any competent manager should be prepared and ready to supply the necessary information.

And yet there is a complication that stands in the way and must first be considered. There is a school of thought which asserts that the 'job', as we have understood it, is on the way out; that its very existence has become a barrier to progress. To set up the 'job', any 'job', could, on this argument, constitute a tacit admission of some failure on the part of management to come to realistic terms with the future.

The alternative proposition is to declare a ban on the highly static concept of 'jobs' and to substitute in its place 'work'. 'What work needs to be done?' can be construed as more practical and focused than asking 'So what's the job?'

Such preferred rewording of the question may sound like a semantic quibble. But there is more to it than that; for the case has been profoundly argued by William Bridges in *Jobshift: How to Prosper in a Workplace without Jobs* (Allen and Unwin, 1995). Bridges takes up the point of Peter Drucker that every organization has to build the management of change into its very structure. 'The difficulty is that the job is proving to be part of the problem not part of the solution . . . Conventional jobs inhibit flexibility and speedy response to threats and opportunities of a rapidly changing market.'

It is a point brought home in the seminal writing of Peter Senge in the *Fifth Discipline* (Doubleday, New York, 1990). His fifth discipline is systems thinking, which flourishes best in the learning organization wherein the whole can exceed the sum of its parts. Here divisions between 'jobs' can obstruct the process of learning. Peter Drucker has taken the point further. In an interview he has cast doubt on the concept of the person who specifies 'jobs', the Manager, preferring to use the word Executive. So too, Michael Hammer, the father of re-engineering, has claimed that 'Middle management, as we currently know it, will simply disappear'.

These pronouncements have a parallel among industrial practitioners. Here leading the way has been Ricardo Semler, captured in his startling but arresting book *Maverick: The World's Most Unusual Workplace* (Arrow, London, 1994). In the flourishing Brazilian company, Semco, job titles, job specifications and many other formalities common in large corporations have been removed as barriers to progress, impediments to cooperation and hindrances to teamwork, while the term Manager has been displaced by a preference for talking about Associates and Coordinators.

These recent developments carry a general message, namely that there is a close connection between the erosion of the concept of the manager and a rejection of jobs as entities in themselves. It is at this latter point, as one looks down at the edge of an abyss, that one questions whether it is wise to take a step forward.

The emptiness of a world without jobs

Work is what all busy people undertake. Its form, outline and purpose give it shape and mould it into what people consider to be their 'job'. Consider the full implications of where the rejection of this basic concept leads. Take the case of a manager, or whatever title may be used in substitution, who wishes to assign work to another. The need to be frank, sincere and open towards the applicant would demand a statement along the following lines:

> No, I must tell you there is no job. We have abolished the notion entirely. All we can offer you is work. None of that work can be guaranteed. It all depends on the market situation and on the interactions of our existing employees in addressing projects and business ventures. Yes, I can understand your sense of insecurity. When starting in new employment it is easy to feel rootless and an outsider unless you have something to cling to, like your own job. But times change. Work is now shared. Its distribution entails breaking into a group of people who know one another well and becoming generally accepted. Then you will find out what you have to do. And, if you prove yourself, you could eventually become established, like some of the others.

I suspect that new employees starting work under such conditions would soon be found to suffer from low morale. One can imagine a search then being made to find new techniques of 'motivation'. Yet the best motivator of all is intrinsic in a job a person can call his or her own; which creates a sense of personal identity and entails that exchange of reciprocal services that lies at the heart of every thriving enterprise.

However indefinite the job, it is more than a task or a set of tasks. A job is the favoured currency for describing the self in communicating with another in work and in establishing personal standing in a social situation. It is a point that has even been exploited by insightful, decisive but still merciful employers. For example, it is not unusual to find that an executive has been shifted to a position of lower responsibility but with the compensation of an attractive-sounding job. One works manager in a company I used to visit had difficulty in keeping up with the pressures and demands of his work. Thereupon he was transferred to a new position as Director for Special Projects, though no such projects existed. He was delighted with his new elevated title.

Some managers are adept at 'selling' a job because they can create an image with which the individual can identify. Such an approach helps to create contented employees.

However, the issue involves more than psychological factors. Jobs imply structure. The removal of that structure means a loss of bearings. People experience uncertainties on how they should relate to others at work. There is an absence of guidelines on how tasks and responsibilities should be divided. Some structure therefore needs to be retained, though it needs to be shorn of the rigidity with which it has been hitherto associated. Benign hierarchies need to put in place benign structures. Every manager, I would contend, needs to be in a position to say to an applicant for employment and in relation to a stated or unstated question: 'Now let me tell you about the job.'

Dividing jobs in a garden

While the concept of the job has a value in its own right as enhancing the self-image, there is an even more pressing practical argument for the retention of not only the word but also the essential idea. The crux of the matter is what is to happen whenever several people are engaged in the same, similar or adjacent work. If the matter is ignored, all manner of problems can arise. Consider the following simple example.

Like many others, I enjoy gardening and, while my intention had been to look after it solely myself, there comes a point when assistance is required. So I have acquired a gardener, Liam, whose Irish background and roots belong to the land. Liam is never happier than when he is in the garden and given a free hand on what needs to be done: in which context he takes readily to Yellow Work. But unfortunately Liam's main job is that of a driver and the result is that his attendance cannot be guranteed. So from time to time I bring in Fred, a man who had training in some useful trades. But while Fred is always amenable, he insists on knowing precisely what needs doing in the garden. Whenever a difficulty is encountered, he comes knocking at the door for further instructions, which displeases my wife when I am out since she does not know whether she can respond in a way that adequately meets his queries. Fred is happiest when there is plenty of Blue Work around. But, from my point of view, Blue Work needs thinking about more deeply, if it is to be provided in suitably blue form. Nevertheless, I have learned the art of managing in blue and managing in yellow.

While praying that Liam and Fred never arrive together, I have to accept that life does not always go according to plan. The vagaries of Liam's job has meant that he does not always come when expected but can arrive ready for work at some unforeseen time. As misfortune would have it, that can coincide with Fred's attendance. I then have two gardeners and life becomes complicated.

When Gardeners One or Two were on their own, there was no need to elaborate the activities to be undertaken by treating them as a 'job'. But once both gardeners appeared upon the scene, an entirely different situation prevailed. What would Gardener One make of the presence of Gardener Two? And how would Gardener Two react to another behaving in a way that proclaimed a pre-existing claim on and knowledge of the garden? If the two gardeners were not to fall over one another and were to be spared from embarrassment and potential conflict, some separation of their duties would be required.

Here there were several options. One was to make the division of work territorial. Liam could look after the back garden and Fred the front and the side. Unfortunately, their personal skills do not fall out too well along such an artificial dividing line which would, in any case, amplify a seasonal imbalance in their respective workloads. Another solution might be the hierarchical one. Fred could be made the undergardener and that would bring about a means of distributing the work equitably. Such a formula, however, would merely aggravate the problem, for Fred does not see himself in any way as being junior to Liam and would doubtless leave if that solution were thrust upon him. A third option might be to get them to sort it all out themselves, the abdication approach, which one can scarcely see succeeding.

So what other possibilities remain? Here the needs of the work have to be reconciled with the needs of both individuals.

There is now a further consideration that needs to be taken into account. Two people cannot work in the same area without acknowledging each other's existence. Co-existence is best assured within the context of co-working. That raises a design point: work can be designed in a way that either keeps people apart or brings them together. Ideally, therefore, some work needs to be found which lends itself to co-working.

As it happens, for this particular occasion, a suitable activity exists. The large deciduous trees in the garden have dropped a host of leaves which have now spread over the lawns, paths and flowerbeds. The beech leaves can be composted while the leaves from the walnut trees are very resistant to rotting down. Liam is especially good at looking after the garden compost and it is clearly up to him to decide what should go into the compost and what should not. Fred, in turn, has something special to contribute, being the proud possessor of a machine that takes up leaves by vacuum. Now a formula for some combined work is emerging. Fred's machine will suck up the leaves on the flowerbeds and paths, while Liam will tackle the lawn. Together they will load the leaves into the barrow where Liam will separate those leaves destined for composting from those that are not.

Arriving at such an intricate formula that proves mutually satisfactory for both parties takes up a great deal of mental energy. The need to share out the work appropriately in the garden will, I hope, never arise again under current circumstances. However, finding Blue Work for one person and Yellow Work for another is not at all difficult if they are separated in time and space. But bring them together and a whole new set of issues arise.

The difference between work and a job is that while the former may entail miscellaneous activities that may be carried out sporadically and informally, whenever two or more people share a common work area a structure needs to be created. There is then a need to search for concepts and theories about jobs, about the building blocks upon which they are based, about the boundaries dividing one job from another and about the principles that govern those points of contact where they meet. The organization of work soon appears a difficult subject to master, which it is. In the wider world outside the garden great rewards spring from getting it right.

What the candidate wants to know

The arrangement of work is of concern not only to management. When people apply for a job, they are responding to something projected by a job title. They feel it fits and is appropriate. After that comes the matter of what lies behind the job title. For the applicant the meaning of the question 'what is the job?' will differ somewhat from the manager's approach. For the manager it spells dishing out tasks and duties. Any further explanation will focus on conveying knowledge about the business of the company, about its various departments and conditions of employment.

The candidate meanwhile will be harbouring thoughts that, for reasons of diplomacy, remain unspoken:

> Yes, Mr Manager, that's all very well but I also want to know the extent of my physical territory. Will I be staying in one area or have a chance to

move around? Will I have my own desk? Will I have my own office or
be sharing with another? Who will I be seeing most of in my job and how
are we supposed to relate to one another? What will people in my work
area understand about my position? And what am I to understand about
them?

The unspoken answer to this unspoken question, were it to be posed,
would be along the following lines:

Well, Mr Candidate, I am surprised you have the temerity to ask such
questions. We will show you in due course. Or perhaps it would be truer
to say you will be thrown in at the deep end and you will have to work
out relationships for yourself. There is a sort of pecking order at work.
Those who have been here longest largely determine the sort of informal
relationships to which you refer. It is a question of custom and practice.
The thing to do is to start by acting passively, observe what goes on, and
then try to fit in.

This unstated reply to the foregoing unstated questions would be
counted entirely unsatisfactory were they to be asked. So in practice
not too much is lost by the omission. Protocol prevails. The candidate
remains mute, to which a form of blindness is later added, for the
eventual appointee is left to grope in the dark.

Broadly speaking, the greatest clarity about jobs arises in large
hierarchical institutions which generate a great deal of routine work
(typically Blue Work). The greatest vagueness occurs in high-tech
companies where clever boffins are operating at the leading edge of
technology (typically White Work).

The typicality affects the culture. An organization's culture develops
round its primary work form. Where routine work predominates and
premises have to be opened and closed at precise times, employees are
commended for their smart appearance and duties tend to be specified
and fixed. Where boffins are engaged in the development of a new
product to serve an as yet undeveloped market, which in turn
generates a link with creative advertising, flexitime will be favoured
and people will roll in and out at all sorts of hours. Flamboyance in
dress raises few eyebrows in surprise. In short, anything goes.

Now mix the two cultures and there is a problem. One can scarcely
have rules or customs in one part of the organization that are absent or
forbidden in another. Admittedly, some large organizations display
certain cultural patterns within the totality but these are usually
stratified along seniority lines. They are seen as forms of class
distinction that operate against the sense of togetherness.

To the outsider these issues are obscure. The elite of the newly
graduated are often courted in the universities by prospective
employers pressing the claims of their companies. Yet those who are
sought after will often complain that one company prospectus reads
much like another. What they would like to know is not there. What

are the rules, the customs, the operating values and principles? How are jobs drawn up? How does one move from one job to another? How is teamwork reconciled with individual responsibility?

The main reason why the answers are not given is because the company does not know. This is especially true in the hybrid organization that is neither wholly institutional nor wholly entrepreneurial. The culture is difficult to interpret because it is made up of heterogeneous elements with conflicting facets rendering it it intrinsically unstable. Neither the one party, representing the Establishment, nor the other, representing the Progressive Thrusters, has achieved sufficient dominance to make an indelible mark. The tide of opinion will fluctuate, as first one manager takes the lead and then another. The new recruit must find a way through a maze which is as baffling as that at Hampton Court. Every new starter will feel alone, for the figures who started earlier cannot be clearly seen. How they got to where they are now, wherever that may be, can only be conjectured.

The everyday answer to the question

These unspoken answers to the hypothetical questions I have posed are meant to underline the dilemmas managers face. If managers are to find a way forward, they need a starting point. So it is as well to examine where we are now. At the risk of overgeneralization, I will state nevertheless what I believe to be the usual position.

The plain truth is that managers avoid giving an outside applicant, or even an internal transferee from within the company, the information needed to make a reasonable attack on the job as it has been envisaged. That avoidance is of recent origin; it does not arise out of abdication of duty but out of uncertainty on how to proceed. In the past the matters dealt with were straightforward. Workers were given Blue Work, as we would now classify it, and instructions were precisely given. In Victorian households the servants had duties laid down with a precision that would be unimaginable today. The smallest deviation from those duties would be noticed. The lady and the master of the house could maintain standards through an elaborate disciplinary arrangement operating through a housekeeper, a butler, a head gardener and a gradation of underservants.

As that hierarchy and other hierarchies have withered away, largely for economic reasons, paperwork gradually began to supplant but never to fully replace supervision. Standards slipped. But still the mixed approach of oral and written instructions brought about an adequate standard of competence provided Blue Work remained Blue Work. And then as tasks and responsibilities began to intermingle in the reformed groupings of work now appearing, a new, complicated situation arose. Often the manager could not really know what the job was, especially where its outputs were not entirely visible or its processes could lend themselves to various interpretations. True, there was a need for work to be done but it was often miscellaneous in character. So could it be depicted as a well-defined job? How could it be described? There Bridges is surely right in seeing the artificiality of the approach and sensing the dilemmas to which the concept of a 'job' gave rise.

In the face of such complexities managers have backed away from attempting to convey the nature of a modern job.

Freedom and structure

One lesson that springs from parenthood is that children need both structure and a degree of autonomy. The same, I believe, can be said of employees. But how much freedom and how much structure? That is the question.

The answer ought to depend on the type of work undertaken rather than on rank. Given the philosophy of work set out in the previous chapter, a way forward can be found. Few jobs are monolithic by nature. Most contain more than one type of demand component (or colour set). It is the composition of these sets and their quantitative relativity that determine the essential character of the job and the degree of freedom that is appropriate.

Blue Work represents the highest degree of structure and the lowest degree of autonomy. There is a correct way of doing what has to be done and that allows very little latitude.

White Work offers the greatest freedom because its contribution follows no preordained path. Yet there is no reason why a person should not spend some time bound by the rules of one form of work and another portion of their working time abiding by the rules and practices of the other. The problem of combining two sets of rules lies in the mind. It is not something that people do naturally. But like many other acquired skills it can be learned given the cultivation of self-discipline.

Many managers face just such a need to vary their style of approach when they take the chair at meetings. No longer is it satisfactory to assert a personal view at the outset of a discussion, as when two or three people confer. Consultation needs to start before any personal views are expressed if all parties are to accept that the meeting is well conducted. So, as occurs typically in Orange Work, members of a team will lose that sense of commitment to a decision if they feel it has been imposed on them by a single person.

Where Yellow Work is concerned, one-person decisiveness becomes a valued asset. That same quality is less helpful with Green Work because it is through the sensitive interaction of people that effective work is accomplished. These two qualities are not easily combined in one person but, with a disciplined approach to work, the combination becomes possible.

Once the job is set out, the question arises: can its demands be met? For a satisfactory answer the candidate must know which rules apply in which part of the territory. Through feedback the job-role may be discovered, as eventually it is in most jobs. My gardeners, Liam and Fred, like most workers, could not be sure at the time because I was not sure myself and planning cannot begin until reliable information becomes available. But given eventual knowledge about a lot of Liams and Freds, I would now know how to make a start. One cannot be sure how people will respond but there are now signposts along the route and once the language of these signposts is learned and shared, those in jobs can gain a clearer view of where they are and where they are going.

5

Overcoming initial problems ——

In an optimistic spirit I decided to take advantage of the opportunity that presented itself when talking to an industrial audience on how work might be set up in the future. After a critical analysis of the contemporary scene, I outlined some rudimentary and alternative methods for setting up work and invited volunteers to try them out in their own companies. We were all in a learning situation and could benefit from each other's experience. An experimental approach conducted on a broad scale could set the scene for a significant advance. A number of companies volunteered to take part in the trials, all of which seemed an encouraging start.

While this initiative fell short of an ideal, planned experiment, I expected an orderly outcome that would take the venture forward. But after some weeks a steady trickle of letters began to arrive in our Cambridge office regretting that it had not been possible to progress as planned. The reasons were not clearly stated or were shrouded in notions of 'other pressures'. Behind the polite apologies one suspected there lay unrevealed reasons. What could they be?

There was only one thing for it; it meant delving more deeply into whatever difficulties might be around. In the event the number of problems to be faced and overcome turned out to be greater than we had expected.

A political barrier to innovation

Leaving aside the technical merits or demerits of any proposal containing radical features, the question always to be asked is: what does or would the intended innovation displace?

Here there can be stumbling blocks almost before one starts. Displacement always involves some measure of inconvenience, if not of agony. Methods of setting up, defining and evaluating jobs already exist. If the leading people in Personnel have, as a result of their training, spent much recent time introducing and consolidating conventional procedures in this area, the welcome given to a radical alternative will be less than enthusiastic. The issue goes further than the mere withholding of support. Any member of line management keen to try out some new venture has first to consider whether it is worth the tussle with those having a vested interest in opposing it. The answer to a request for a go-ahead is frequently No, here qualified to the extent that it is not No immediately: it is No eventually. While the attitudinal barrier may be one thing, legitimate political complications are yet another. Objections were sometimes raised about how our proposals would be received at the operating level. Some questions called for reasonable answers. If there have been cuts in the labour force and the workers are feeling insecure, people wonder: is this going to show us up? What guarantee have we that this so-called experiment is not another threat to our job security?

A further roadblock on the path to progress is the possibility of adverse repercussions on an existing payment system, the nature of which needs to be checked out before the next steps are taken. The risks may be minimal or even non-existent in some cases. Some companies, including Japanese-owned companies in particular, have broad-banded payment systems: changing the boundaries of the job is unlikely to affect the take-home pay.

Other companies have narrow-banded systems of payment based on intricate systems of job evaluation. Here any change is liable to have serious consequences. Once that prospect has been mulled over by management, 'no further action' will be the probable safety-first decision. It was a fair estimate that the greatest economic gains resulting from Workset are likely in companies with narrow-banded systems of payment. Yet, paradoxically, these are also the very places where, due to entrenched interests, the greatest opposition is to be expected.

Whether objections are attitudinal or have a rational economic basis, the effect is much the same: the amount of energy and courage needed by executives to push something through is usually greater than that which seems justified when their in-trays contain other priorities.

Seeds scattered on stony ground do not readily germinate. But with good fortune there is always fertile soil to be found somewhere, provided one searches long enough. Whether it was a matter of chance or a reward for sensitive antennae, we had enough industrial contacts to arrive eventually at a spot where the political conditions were right, where those in Personnel had an innovative and progressive outlook, and where doubts had already begun to enter the minds of senior managers about the advisability of clinging to conventional policies. Now placed in a more favourable situation, we were ready to face the next obstacle.

Communicating about the unfamiliar

The first good opportunity to try out the proposed system in a company well disposed towards experimentation began well enough. An outline of the project to the manager in charge of the chosen operational area, along with the subsequent discussion, took about an hour and a half. Such a period seems a fair investment of a busy manager's time if the same person is to supervise the setting up of several jobs. The real difficulty lay in what to say to the workers. The presentation needed to be much briefer and to the point. The more we rehearsed our lines, the less convincing it all sounded.

I do not know whether it is a characteristic of the British industrial worker or merely industrial workers in all countries, but the verbal elaborations that are a necessary part of explanation tend to arouse suspicion and misgivings. The educated are seen as wordspinners, out of touch with everyday realities, and prone to impose on working people ideas that fail to make sense when put to the practical test. It is a barrier that has to be overcome whenever radical changes need to be made to working practices.

The key to progress at the workplace often lies in throwing away preconceptions and starting by engaging in an act of empathy, that is, by trying to envisage how people are likely to feel about what is proposed. After a number of discussions we came to the conclusion that it would be better to start with no assumptions. So we formulated the beguilingly simple, and yet bold, decision to desist at the outset from any prepared and definite explanation.

Instead, the plan set out the various items of work on differently coloured sheets of paper. These differences in colour would be assumed to have some meaningful significance. The recipient of the information could make inferences or discuss it with chosen colleagues and workmates or, if the mystery needed to be cleared up, could ask questions. Extra bits of information would then be fed in as required.

The generic title for this approach is the Guided Discovery Method of Training. I had used it with good effect much earlier in my career when working as a consultant for OECD in setting up training programmes for unemployed older workers in member countries*. The point about the method is that people can assimilate whatever is to be learned at their own pace. When they need more information and clarification they can ask for it. Gradualism can work where direct instruction and exhortation fail. The method offers a great deal of rope but should not be confused with abdication from responsiblity for

The Discovery Method: An International Experiment in Retraining, No. 6 in series Employment of Older Workers, OECD Publications, 1969. Also *The Discovery Method in Training*, Training Services Agency, HMSO, 1969.

training. The Discovery Method, or to give it its full name the Guided Discovery Method, benefits from more careful planning than its name might imply. If there is a general principle that suitably conveys the essence of the method, it is that it is better to give too little information than too much. Rather than massing information at the start of learning, the passage of information is extended over time. In this way more of the essential content is absorbed.

Using such a strategy in negotiations with managers would be out of the question. To hold back on information is scarcely an option. Managers will usually decline to participate in any new venture until they are fully aware of what is required, understand the theory and agree with the purpose. Reluctant managers will oppose, whereas reluctant workers will show indifference and fail to cooperate. The latter problem is more elusive in that it is not clear whether a problem exists or not. Only time will tell. Here that possibility and the consequences to which it may lead should never be overlooked or underrated. That is why our greatest concern now became the jobholders. In due course we would need to extract information about their response to the briefings. What processes and procedures were needed? What would be the overall attitude of the jobholders to the general direction in which we were trying to move?

Enter the facilitator

The first introductory exercises into classifying work the new way took place during all-day seminars attended by managers and personnel professionals. Participants were grouped into teams in order to tackle the exercises. If any evidence were needed that people differ, this was it. Some groups completed the exercise with consummate skill. In dissecting familiar jobs they transposed formal categorizations into new insightfully conceived entities appropriate to the colour codings. Other groups merely assigned a colour to traditional breakdowns of the job in a mechanistic and thoughtless fashion. The spirit of the exercise was alive in some groups, totally absent in others. There were some individuals who from that moment onwards jumped to see all aspects of jobs in colour codes. They acted as pupils well ahead of their tutors.

Here there was a reminder of an industrial lesson that has been authenticated on many occasions: that the problems of adult learning are more connected with unlearning that which no longer applies than with picking up what is new. Here familiarity with job analysis and job specifications often proved more of a hindrance than an advantage. Were it not for the fact that a few pupils were evidently so much ahead of the class, the difficulties would have looked forbidding.

Some hopeful pointers now emerged on the next steps to be taken. Trials aimed at reforming the way in which jobs were set up needed a few suitable pioneers. These pioneers were typically training officers who had previously been bogged down in routine activities and now saw a chance of doing something exciting and new.

In a field where pitfalls abound progress inevitably depends on technique and experience. That experience can be condensed and made available to others starting out for the first time. The general strategy was to make information about the system available at three levels of depth; the deepest in the case of facilitators, at average depth for the managers and at the shallowest depth for jobholders. It is not that one group was deliberately deprived of the requisite information and guidance: rather, experience showed that there was a preferred depth of water in which the group liked to swim.

Since the facilitators needed something more comprehensive than the others, the chosen means of meeting this need was to compile a Facilitator's Manual. The creation and very existence of such a manual may convey the impression that the facilitator was being presented with Blue Work. The manual did, it was true, spell out procedures; but it was not a blueprint; it was not a document to be followed slavishly by the fledgling facilitator. Rather, the purpose of the manual was to place on record what had already been learned. The facilitators who took part in the early experiments were characteristically the sort of people who would have ignored Blue Work anyway and who would have found White Work more engaging. But it did not matter. The manual was a growing document to which facilitators could contribute. And through that contribution they grew in commitment.

The manual opened with the concept of the overall plan and of the benefits it could offer, set out the types of work that fell into the various colour codes, gave hints on the more difficult decisions in classification and suggested ways in which the facilitator might work with the manager to best advantage.

Once the principles were agreed the writing of the manual proved straightforward and a lot was accomplished in a short period of time. The pace then began to slow. A large hurdle loomed in the path of further progress. The vitality of the system depended on receiving feedback from the jobholder about certain essentials. These included which parts of the overall job had occupied the jobholder's time, which parts had occupied less time than the manager supposed, and what new work had been performed that lay outside the jobholder's original briefing. None of this information could spring to life without putting some meaningful figures around these various categories.

Jobholders are reluctant estimators. Estimating is, after all, a separate profession, well recognized and established in the engineering industry. One could hardly expect a jobholder to take over an estimator's work. Self-estimation, moreover, was especially difficult in this context. The distinction between Blue and Yellow Work is clear in many cases. For example, a nurse will carry out the routine activities in administering pills (Blue Work) at the behest of the doctor who takes over responsibility for the patient's treatment (Yellow Work). But what would happen in the case of the surgeon who is responsible for the outcome of the surgical operation but is also carrying the finer parts of the work himself? The two activities would overlap in time.

This overlapping in time presented a problem in a number of industrial activities in which our jobholders were found to be engaged. Yet somehow these different aspects of the work needed to be disentangled and fed into the feedback loop in quantitative terms. Such data were vital if detection in personal shifts in workload and activity were to yield leads of value for job realignment and career development. It was at this point that we suffered a prolonged halt while we endeavoured to find a system capable of providing reliable figures that could offer leads for action. But eventually that hurdle was overcome and we were able to recommence the journey. How that came about will be covered in Chapter 9.

6

Job casting and job briefing —

So how do you want the job set up? This is a question that managers find arresting, for it implies that options are available, as indeed they are.

The first decision to be made is what to include and what to exclude in the job: which is the province of Job Casting. For many managers this has scarcely been seen as a problem. The various elements are put together on the basis of logical convenience or the shape of the job is taken from traditional practice. Take two cases, a sales representative and a hospital physician. The duties of the former typically include opening up new contacts, persuading customers about the merits of the company's products, administering any orders, ensuring delivery is as scheduled and checking that the customer is satisfied with what is received. In the case of the hospital physician the position seems equally clear-cut. The physician 'owns' given patients, secures a bed for them and is responsible for both their treatment and discharge when that treatment has been completed.

But the position in both cases is more complicated than it looks. Take the sales representative. Selling skills embody special aptitudes. The successful salesperson is usually adept at Green Work and likes a briefing containing a substantial portion of Yellow. The downside is often poor performance with anything containing a spot of Blue. The consequence can be that good sales are achieved but customers feel let down. This combination of a plus and a minus is hardly a satisfactory outcome. Setting up the job of a sales representative in its rounded form is often not the best solution. An alternative can be to cast the job in two parts, giving the selling part to one person and the administrative part to another, while ensuring the two work in close harmony.

The position of the hospital physician is more complicated in both its medical and political dimensions. Illnesses do not always parcel themselves neatly into the province of the solo specialist. Others may have to be consulted. When it comes to discharge, a number of considerations have to be taken into account and in the best hospitals this becomes a subject for Orange Work. The physician could at that point feel he has 'lost' his patient whom he views as part of his Yellow Work and will resent the intrusion into his area of responsibility. In the absence of colour clarification and understanding of the theory of jobs, the fact that the boundaries have changed will not be apparent. Tension will mount between the two 'sides' without necessarily showing itself as open conflict. Incompatible powers and incompatible views operate side by side but avoid exposure in the interest of pursuing a quiet life. Nevertheless, I feel that in the long run the failure to come to terms with the real position must be damaging.

Much of the problem springs from the tendency for the manager to back away from management. Instead of the manager being 'someone who assigns tasks and responsibilities to others', other functions take precedence, since managers seldom usually have a duality of duties, doubling as executives or professionals with a certain amount of important personal work to perform. A good executive may make a poor manager, because not much time is spent on work that is truly managerial. My aim is to bring managerial work back to managers. That means creating greater involvement in the business of 'assigning work to others'.

While the entry of the facilitator was planned to make that aim easier to accomplish, I never intended that the facilitator should take over the basic responsibility that belongs to the manager. It is, of course, tempting for the manager to back away and say 'You seem to know a lot about it, so I will leave it to you'. Managers do delegate. But delegating in this field is tantamount to abdication from the essence of their job.

The role of the facilitator is to collect and present information and to pose the relevant questions which the manager will have to answer. The facilitator may have a covert educational role to play in relation to the manager. That role is transitional because one system is crumbling but still in place, while another is moving into position but has not fully arrived. Eventually the manager should be in a position to act with a greater sense of autonomy, will not wait for prompting and will recognize the benefits of assigning work with more discrimination than in the past.

The manager will say 'Let me now consider, how do I want this job set up?

Preparing a brief for innovation

Take the case of a company that has enjoyed the benefits of a long-running product that now has a limited life. There is nothing ready to take its place. If the manager is to address this issue with a constructive initiative, a job or jobs will need to be set up in an appropriate way and suitable people assigned to carry out the work. Given the fact that there are some resources available within the company, how should the manager start in the light of the approach that is favoured?

The first priority must be to avoid the mistake commonly made in companies with products having a high technical or scientific content. In such companies many of the scientific and technical employees are likely to have duties embodying a great deal of routine testing, the nature of which is typically Blue Work. Because they possess the necessary expertise and a suitable technical background these employees are likely to be assigned to new product development. Unfortunately, long-standing experience in Blue Work produces an outlook that does not harmonize well with new creative ventures. Those recruited with the appropriate credentials but who in a personal sense did not feel comfortable with Blue Work will have departed for jobs offering greater scope for self-expression. That leaves those now positioned to start the new creative venture as the ones least suited to make a success of it.

Better results could be expected by detailing for such a venture individuals who have already made their mark in Yellow Work, or by setting the job in a way that would fit Green Workers or by treating it as an Orange Work assignment.

At the beginning the facilitator will say to the manager: 'You have some options here.' 'Explain to me,' replies the manager, 'what these options are in terms of how the job can be set up'.

'Well,' says the facilitator, 'take the case of someone currently engaged in Yellow Work, who thrives on the opportunities it creates and has performed well. We can consider that person, whom we will call Y, to take charge of some new venture. Look here, Y, we will say, the aim of your new job is to find a new product. You can develop one within the company or you can bring one in under licence. We don't really care so long as it replaces the product that is fading, starts to bring in an income and makes a profit. We will discuss a budget and a time span within which you are expected to produce results. That's the long and the short of it, Y. So do you want the job?'

'I think I know a Y who would grab an opportunity like this.'

'That could be the very person we need.'

'But how,' wonders the manager, 'could we set up the job for Green Workers?'

'We would do it informally. We would explain that the company needs a new product. Discuss it among yourselves. And if anyone has ideas, bring them forward and we will give you time off from your current job to take any prospective venture forward. Even without that invitation there is a possibility that any employee might come up with the germ of an idea that could not be advanced individually but which could progress with the support of others. Such initiatives would arise in the form of White Work, constituting White Work because it is not part of the briefing for their job. To carry an intitiative forward, the next step is probably to set up Orange Work and to design a well-balanced team for the purpose. Another option is to approach it through Yellow Work where the initiative is more restricted in scope and application.'

'If we can develop a culture that helps to foster initiatives, that is all to the good. But we cannot live on hope. Suppose we want a more definite attack on the problem?'

'That is where the job needs to be set up in the first place as Orange Work.'

'So how do we start?'

'We first need to decide who to have in a new venture team. We can draft in selected people who can work part-time, combining this responsibility with the duties of their existing job. Getting the balance of the team right is crucial. Equally vital is the education of the team members in understanding their own team roles and those of each other. We then leave them to it. The team is then empowered.'

'How is this worded under the briefing?'

'It is simplicity itself. The wording on the Orange sheet of the Workset briefing will say: You are appointed a member of the new venture team. This body will be collectively responsible for finding and introducing one or more new products by the year . . .'

The manager may wonder which of these three approaches is to be preferred. A choice has to be made between Yellow and Orange Work. Otherwise there would be trouble and conflict between two parties charged with the same goal and approaching it from different angles. In the case of Green Workers, there is less situation risk. For them, work on new ventures is an incidental activity, for which provision is made, without being the prime focus of their job briefing. Any success gained in this area would be an unexpected spin-off from a social process. Once spotted, it could be elevated into a submission to be taken forward by Y, if that option for approaching a new venture was chosen by the manager; or it would be referred to an empowered team if the Orange approach was favoured. 'So which should it be?' the manager may muse.

The facilitator must take the line: 'It's your decision. You will know your people and the circumstances best.'

Setting up the job

Dubbing workers with particular colours is a useful shorthand to be employed in the light of experience and in conversations among the cognoscenti. In reality no-one need be dubbed in advance. No presumption is or should be made. When a briefing is prepared the manager has to take two immediate factors into consideration:

1 What parts of the work hang together so that it is sensible for them to be performed by a single person?
2 Which aspects of the work need to be teased apart and then reassembled and subsumed in one of the four core colour categories?

Any job may therefore come out with a briefing that incorporates each of the four core colour codes. Added latitude is supplied by the general briefing allowing the jobholder to feed back information in terms of the seven colour codes available. Only then does the personal inclination of the jobholder stand out (see Chapter 8). Only then can a jobholder be described as inclining to a particular colour in working style. That emerging colour will influence the realignment of the job and the career development of the jobholder.

The mixed colour briefing makes no presumptions about the working style of the appointee other than about general suitability for the position.

A major feature of the skill in writing up the brief lies in the wording of the work elements. Blue Work needs to be spelt out in detail. Standards and specifications should be incorporated wherever possible. These invite interventions by training and supervision in order to ensure that those who undertake the work are qualified and competent and that agreed standards are maintained and laid-down procedures are being followed. Green Work has a less structured character so the various items are best treated in generic terms. The common feature of Green Work is that its tasks depend on circumstances and on people. For a community nurse, training may provide a useful background but will offer no prescribed approach. Each case is best handled as it comes and will demand social discretion. Certain manual work has a similar character, where the execution of the task depends on the immediate situation. For example, a builder's labourer provides a service to others on a building site and proficiency in the job is likely to depend not so much on how correctly the cement is mixed (that is taken for granted) as on how well demands are anticipated. Here it is important that the right materials arrive at the right place at the right time. Good performance depends on responding to the needs of the bricklayer and on communication. Most Green Work has a social connection: its character is influenced by what someone else does or says. Hence the social nature of this category of work generates its own immediate reactive demands. That exempts any need to specify in advance exactly what and how the work is to be carried out. A generic description of these tasks will adequately set the scene.

Yellow Work is the easiest type of work to set up since the only requirement is a statement of the objectives. Here a comparison may be drawn with management by objectives – a much-favoured means of setting up managerial work. Non-managerial work can be set up in similar fashion. Even a person in a comparatively lowly job can be treated as fully capable of deciding how a job is to be tackled once the aim is made clear. Treating people with respect in this way, especially where it has long been lacking, improves morale and increases satisfaction in the job.

Orange Work also needs little in the way of specification. The emphasis falls more on defining an orbit of collective operation and responsibility. With whom should a person collaborate in decision making and to what end? There could be only one person involved or there could be several. Orange Work could be broadly defined as 'Yellow Work for Teams'. Such an area of shared endeavour is very susceptible to misunderstanding. Hence clarity rather than effort becomes the watchword. In setting the work up the focus should fall on ensuring that those involved all see the same picture. It is a process often better handled by talking to people than by getting it right on paper. The paperwork should preferably follow as a ratification of what has already been agreed.

Once the essential differences between the four different types of work have been fully comprehended and the principles of the colour coding accepted, the manager and the facilitator can confer on how the work is best distributed.

Most people are likely to welcome a bit of each colour since for them variety is the spice of life. Blue Work may be fine in a limited measure but social needs at work have also to be met. The possiblity that the jobholder can also use three additional colours, Grey, White and Pink, for purposes of feedback needs to be explained and can add to the interest of the job challenge. However, there are many exceptions. Some show a marked preference for work of one colour and an aversion to that of another colour. A 'rainbow' formula has therefore to be ruled out for those whose work inclination has already taken on a pronounced pattern. A third group that deserves special attention consists of those whose inclination towards a particular colour work form does not gain an adequate outlet in the current job.

To sum up, the work has to be right for appointees in that they will feel fulfilled by what the job demands. Equally, there has to be assurance that appointees will interpret their assignments in the way required.

Presenting a brief

Once the decision is made and a job is drawn up, the person to whom the job is assigned needs to be won over, if consultation has not already taken place. Gaining support for a scheme that is radically different cannot be presumed, for people often find it difficult to depart from the expected. In the past the position has been clear-cut. The workers would await instruction: they would expect a boss to behave like a boss, even if they cavilled at the autocratic style. The success of any departure from this conventional paradigm depends on creating a new understanding.

The crucial point to be put across is the difference between a briefing and an instruction, the essence of which lies not in the message but in the relationship. That is why the facilitator is not the person to convey the change in relationship implicit in the briefing; that change can only be communicated by the manager, because the primary relationship is between the manager, who assigns work to others, and the jobholders: the facilitator is merely an enabler.

The manager should be saying something like this:

> We are trying to change our approach to assigning work. In future, we are going to give you a brief rather than an instruction. This means a real change of system which will result in your having more say on how the job develops. You will receive a brief written on sheets marked with four different colours, according to whether we are asking you to undertake tasks or responsibilities, to work on your own or with others. Only in the case of the blue sheets will we expect you to carry out the work exactly in the way required. We are leaving it to you to decide how to allocate your time between these different duties. You are in the best position to judge. All we ask is that from time to time you let us know how it is working out. We will be giving you some sheets on which you can write your returns.

If this statement were followed by no more than a nod of acknowledgement, it would be a speech. What is required is not a speech but a dialogue. Only if the jobholder responds can one be convinced that real change is on the way; that jobholders are replacing 'workers'.

Only after the dialogue has run its course and created the right atmosphere will the facilitator be in a position to enter more fully into the scene and to furnish more information about procedures and prospects. The grey sheets will invite the recording of peripheral work called for by responding to the general demands of the job itself without having been mentioned specifically within the four core work assessment sheets. White Work will be explained as covering other work which the jobholder has seen as worth doing. This is discovered work. Such work comes about only through the use of personal initiative but it has not in a sense been sanctioned since it lies outside the job casting. The pink sheets cover what is known as time spent in attendance, such time generating no useful outputs in tasks accomplished or responsibilities fulfilled. Interruptions, waiting time and wasted time all come into this category. Yet it is likely that the time being squandered is not the fault of the jobholder, providing time has not been diverted from the core work. Pink Work is a function of the way contingencies and external factors impinge on the job. The existence of these factors affords an opportunity for the facilitator to bring out the possibilities of expanding and changing personal role boundaries. The white and the pink, in particular, allow the jobholder to notice what is missing from the job and what needs to be done to bring about improvements. The pink flags up time that could be better spent. The white shows that even without further briefing time has already been put to good use. A large amount of Grey Work allows the jobholder to draw attention to the volume of incidental activities that surround the core area and possibly detract from attention to the main business of the job.

The jobholder can complete the circle of communication by feeding back to his or her manager how the job is going and thus influence the next briefing. The process of communication calls for delicately balanced skills and, because it occupies perhaps the most critical part of the chain, the chain is most susceptible to being fractured at this point. That underscores the importance of the chapter that follows.

7

Improving communications ———

In large-scale organizations the drawing up of a job usually entails an assembly of procedures directed at the intended worker who stands at the far end of a downward communication chain. Once the message has reached its destination the journey is over. It would then be out of order for the worker to depart from the written terms of reference. There is no further room for discussion before a considerable lapse of time. Eventually the worker is in a position to respond to what has been laid down by the job specification under the formalities attached to annual appraisals. However, the appropriate paperwork is primarily designed to account for any failure to achieve the written objectives, and precludes the opportunity for making a more proactive response.

In contrast, Workset embarks on a different mission. Its aim is to produce a regular flow of information about the job that moves up as well as down. The system is designed to enhance the quality of that information and to regulate its quantity. Too much information would defeat the purpose: it would then become a burden and act merely as a generator of noise in the system. Insufficient information, or information without relevance to actions that can be taken, would inevitably be ignored. A new facility in terms of a special language has to be built in to streamline communication. The price that has to be paid for this intervention is the time taken to acquire the language; but, once acquired, the language steadily gains in meaning with continued use. The key to the control of this new system of communication lies with a specialist intermediary, the facilitator, whose aim is to improve the flow of useful information and to supervise the inputs and the outputs. In that way the messages conveyed have a better prospect of becoming clear to all parties.

Under Workset there are three players, the facilitator (F), the manager (M) and the jobholder (J). The initial function of F is to help M to set up the job for J, an activity for which M has prime responsibility. F will have been educated in the philosophy and technology of Workset and therefore will be in a position to explain how Workset operates and what benefits can be expected. F acts as the close partner of M in the initial step of work assessment, prompting questions to which M supplies the answers. The operations of F reduces M's workload, so freeing M to concentrate on those key activities that lie at the core of the job of the manager or belong to its necessary ramifications. Certainly, a prerequisite for the successful functioning of F is that M sees the goal of the approach as worth while. Whether that happens or not depends on a policy decision by the corporate body of management rather more than it does on any spontaneous relationship between one particular F and one particular M. But once that hurdle of collective decision making is overcome and the go-ahead is given, facilitators and managers are well placed to work together in a state of harmony and alliance.

The real challenge for the facilitator then begins. Here the key to ultimate success lies in enabling Fs to communicate effectively with Js, the ultimate point of which is to facilitate the communication of Js with Ms. The means by which this subtle, if convoluted, route is pursued now becomes the central issue. When viewed from afar, it might almost appear as if there was no need for a third party. Js would certainly favour anyway the idea of commenting on the brief they receive, of feeding back to the manager information on how the job is working out, of commenting on how time is spent, on how often it is wasted for reasons beyond his control, and of flagging up any initiatives J may have taken. Ideally, many Js would prefer in a perfect world to tell Ms to their face rather than act through an agent. 'What I have always wanted to say to the boss is . . .'

Yet this ideal picture is something of a fantasy. There is no real prospect that M would be in a position to take over the role of F either on grounds of availability or of being able to cope with all the technicalities. On the one hand, M will lack F's professional advantage in training for this specialist role; and, on the other, Ms have their own set of priorities from which they are reluctant to be diverted. Talking to the person in the job may occur during normal business. That is fine as far as it goes. Yet any dialogue is bound to take place in a structured setting which inevitably limits its value. A free exchange of opinions could offer more but would be difficult to set up without risking labyrinthine discussions; which is exactly what a manager is anxious to avoid.

The case of the ordered sandwiches

In an early trial of a feedback system, and in the spirit of wanting to learn more, we explored the differences between the job as seen by the manager and the job as seen by the jobholder and, since delicate issues could be involved, a dummy run was considered desirable. In one establishment it was deemed that the safest course would be to try things out on a personnel assistant in the central personnel department. Stacey was accordingly selected for having an amiable and cooperative disposition. The conditions of this trial meant that any blunders made were least likely to have unfavourable repercussions.

Once the job had been assessed and broken down in terms of the colour sets, we sought to study the quality and nature of the feedback from J. Stacey had already received a copy of the reclassified breakdown of her job and had in any case become familiar with the job under an original job specification.

But now she was given the colour sheets with blank items; which signified that Stacey, as the jobholder, should fill in the elements of the job as she saw them. Stacey had already conferred with her manager about the job over a period of time. It was therefore no surprise that there was a good deal of agreement about the items on the blue sheets. But was unexpected was the number of items on the yellow sheets.

One item in particular struck us as a little odd. It said 'Getting sandwiches'. How, we asked ourselves, could the fetching of sand-wiches be interpreted as an assigned goal or objective for the achievement of which J was held individually accountable? If the division between a task and a responsibility was clearly understood, it could only be a task. It could not even be counted a blue task, since the task did not involve a specified standard to which the jobholder should work. Possibly it could be seen as a green task arising out of an interaction between two people. 'Get me some sandwiches, Stacey.' 'The usual?' 'Yes, fine.' But it was scarcely a requirement that would normally find its way into any sort of job description.

On our own estimation it was a typical piece of Grey Work. So we taxed Stacey with the reasons for her classification. The conversation preceding the ordering of the sandwiches had not taken the course we had envisaged. The original order had, allegedly, carried a different message. It was something like 'Get me some better sandwiches'. Apparently sandwiches ordered on some previous occasion had not been very satisfactory. Therefore, Stacey reasoned, she was being presented with an objective against which she would be judged. Inevitably, the sandwiches would now reach the desired standard or would fail to do so. Hence there was a case for classifying this assignment as Yellow Work.

Faced with this unarguable logic, we were thrown into a state of temporary perplexity. Were our plans to be defeated by these sandwiches? While the incident itself might be seen as inconsequential, conceivably, it could have a broader significance. Could it be that the way in which people understand words is so idiosyncratic that proper communication can never be guaranteed?

It was this suspect weakness that now provided some clue on how we should best proceed. Stacey had written the word 'getting',

CONTRASTS IN COMMUNICATION

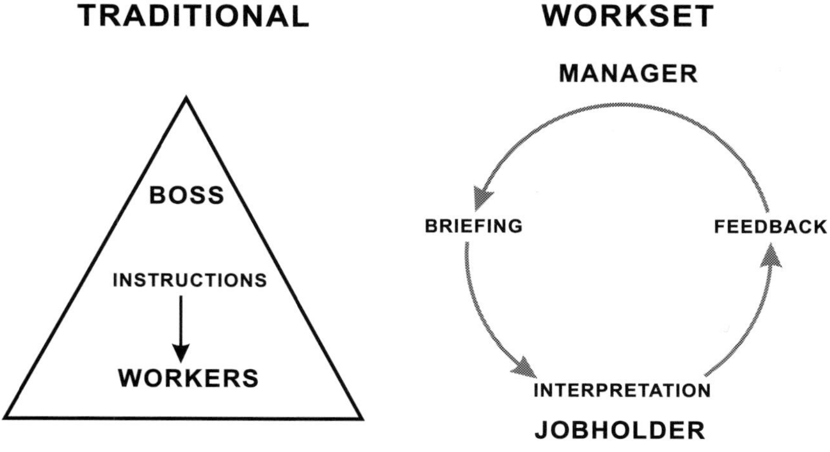

TRADITIONAL

WORKSET

BOSS

INSTRUCTIONS

WORKERS

MANAGER

BRIEFING

FEEDBACK

INTERPRETATION

JOBHOLDER

SETTING UP THE JOB WITH AND WITHOUT FEEDBACK

Plate 5

EXPLANATION OF WORKSET COLOUR SETS

 **Blue Work** refers to tasks that a Jobholder has to carry out in a prescribed way to an approved standard.

Example: Machining an engineering component to a specification with tight tolerances.

 Green Work refers to tasks that can vary according to the reactions and needs of others.

Example: Helping the hotel services manager at times of peak occupancy.

Yellow Work involves individual responsibility for meeting an objective. Exactly how the work is done does not matter too much as long as the goal is achieved.

Example: Initiating procedures to reduce re-working costs by 15% over the next 12 months.

 Orange Work involves shared rather than individual responsibility for achieving the objective.

Example: Co-ordinating a management team in a hospital where policies are needed for making better use of limited resources.

 Grey Work relates to work that is incidental to the job. It has much in common with Green Work in so far as it often involves responding to situational needs. Grey Work however is not formerly covered by duties described in any of the four core categories of Workset.

Example: A secretary is diverted to help another executive with matters not covered in a job definition.

White Work has to do with any new or creative undertaking that lies outside the Jobholder's formal duties but which can or does lead to improvements.

Example: A salesperson analyses what influences customers when deciding to place repeat orders and as a result devises a new telephone follow-up procedure.

 Pink Work demands the presence of the Jobholder but leads to no useful results. Time is considered by the Jobholder to be largely wasted.

Example: A Jobholder is regularly required to attend meetings where nothing new is learnt and no contribution to decision making is encouraged.

Plate 6

THE DYNAMICS OF WORKSET

An Interactive Model

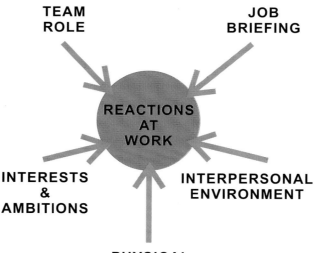

TEAM
ROLE

JOB
BRIEFING

REACTIONS
AT
WORK

INTERESTS
&
AMBITIONS

INTERPERSONAL
ENVIRONMENT

PHYSICAL
ENVIRONMENT

THE EFFECTS OF ORDERS AND INSTRUCTIONS. ONLY BY DISCOVERING WHAT ACTUALLY HAPPENS AT THE WORKPLACE CAN OPERATIONS BE WELL MANAGED.

Plate 7

THE SKILLS FOCUS OF WORKSET

ABILITY TO PLAY A KEY ROLE IN A TEAM

INDIVIDUAL DECISION-MAKING CAPACITY

INTERPERSONAL SENSITIVITY

COMPETENCES

ADAPTABILITY

CREATIVE ABILITY

A BROAD OUTLOOK

*DIFFERENT PERSONAL SKILLS COME TO THE FORE
AS THE FOCUS OF THE JOB CHANGES*

Plate 8

probably one of the most indefinite words in the English language. In conjunction with a variety of adverbs and nouns its meanings change as startlingly as a chameleon. Could it be that the loose use of language is a barrier to communication? Could that be the true function of jargon? That it ties meaning down to the interlocutors, so excluding risks of ambiguity? An additional hazard is that loose language confuses the self. The self may fail to follow meaning because the self translates what is heard into a more familiar internal language. The loss in translation and the lack of anchor for effective recall then increases the extent of the space separating current cognition from the message originally relayed. So people end up being tripped up by words.

The lesson of the sandwiches now came under review. Suppose that the chief executive had expressed dissatisfaction with the sandwich arrangements prevailing in the company and had detailed someone to improve them. How should that assignment have been expressed?

Due clarity could have been preserved had the inscription on the yellow sheet read 'Investigate local suppliers of sandwiches and make recommendations'. It is not, of course, the type of entry likely to be found on a job briefing. Every job has its core items and no jobholder is likely to find the 'getting of sandwiches' included in any sort of job definition. But trivial as the incident may seem, the lesson of the sandwiches contributed to the further development of the system. It caused us to bring into being Grey Work, covering all those incidental activities that spin off from and do not merit recording as core work, but which at the same time are not innovative enough to count as White Work or futile enough to be seen as Pink Work.

A dictionary of workset verbs

Language needs to be used in a disciplined way if it is to be put to good use in effective communication. Indeed we found evidence that the use of language was becoming a barrier to progress in this case not only of jobholders but of managers too. During exercises conducted in the course of seminars, managerial groups were asked to analyse the make-up of some job with which they were familiar and then to compose and enter the defining sentences on the appropriate colour sheets. The exercise was undertaken in an accomplished way by some groups. But among other groups misunderstandings had clearly arisen. Some of the entries were no more than items lifted from conventional job descriptions and reclassified into what were considered their appropriate colour sets without any further modification. The wording was treated almost as a secondary matter.

After further analysis, the distinction between the groups that had undertaken the exercise with insight and those that had brought nothing to the exercise largely revolved round the choice of verbs, if indeed a verb had been used at all. A well-chosen verb would yield a real message as to how the job should be approached. Some verbs fell naturally into a colour set, while others would stretch across colour sets and would therefore be conducive to varied interpretations. For example, 'carrying out duties . . .' would be meaningless in Workset terms.

The plan for facilitating communication between the manager and the jobholder now took shape. To assist in understanding 'how' a job should be approached a list of approved verbs was drawn up that had natural affinity with a given colour set. For example, 'instructing' was a natural for blue. The notion of an instruction implies that a definite method is being imparted and that there is a correct way of doing things. 'Educating', however, belongs in yellow, since the educator is choosing a path to a goal in a situation where the ultimate goal itself is clearly envisaged, although the tasks and procedures for getting there may vary. 'Negotiating' sounds similar but the reality is very different. If two people without a common objective pursue the two separate paths to two separate goals, there is in effect no negotiation. Modern negotiation follows the route of win–win, the interactive nature of which turns it into Green Work. On the other hand, given the need to accomplish a fixed goal the business of negotiating is better described as 'selling': in the context of commission selling, it falls into Yellow Work. 'Conferring' would be the preferred choice of word where a group of people meet for the purpose of pursuing a common objective and in that context the verb signifies Orange Work.

Debating the meaning of words could easily become an unrewarding activity. Summoning up verbs and constructing sentences around them can be a time-consuming and error-prone process. Nevertheless words have a vital role to play in communication and the problem had to be addressed. Selecting words from a given list proved to reduce greatly the stringency of the exercise together with the time it occupied. Examples of the recommended verbs are given in Table 7.1.

The major benefit of the list of approved verbs was that, without further explanation, it assisted the comprehension of the jobholder. Whether a portion of work was a task or a responsibility, or a matter solely for the individual or to be shared, now received a double cue: there was the colour and the verb. Taken together they supplied the answer to the imaginary question: 'But how? By following the approved procedure (blue plus suitable verb): by responding to the needs of the moment (green plus suitable verb): by deciding how best to undertake the responsibility for which you are personally accountable (yellow plus suitable verb): by reaching decisions through teamwork (orange plus suitable verb).'

Table 7.1 Examples of verbs used in job casting (extracted from the *Facilitator's Manual*)

Blue Work	administering, applying, checking, inputting, implementing, machining, measuring, registering, scheduling
Yellow Work	advising, deciding, designing, forecasting, lecturing, organizing, recommending, revising, selling (on commission)
Green Work	answering, assisting, interviewing, negotiating, reassuring, seeking, supporting, visiting, welcoming
Orange Work	conferring, contributing, co-ordinating, integrating, orchestrating, participating, policy-making, proposing, sharing (problems)

Formulating the return message

Now it became the jobholder's turn to communicate back to the originator of the briefing. One aspect of the communication covered the extent to which the briefing, as envisaged by the manager, was being put into practice. A time key occupied one part of the jobholder's assessment sheet for each of the four colours and comprised boxes that were struck off to indicate the time spent on that item. The time keys did not denote a pre-fixed time period, for it was left to the jobholder to decide on the reference period governing the sampling of the work. Sometimes the time key would refer to units of half an hour and sometimes to units of ten minutes. At any rate once account had been taken of the selected reference period the number of struck-off boxes could be counted and turned into time and into the percentage of time spent on work of varying types. Sometimes an item specified by the manager occupied zero time because the anticipated work had not arrived. Other items would indicate that large amounts of time had been spent. Where work is made up of bits and pieces, which is the modern trend, no-one can predict with any degree of certainty how time is going to be employed during any given period. The important thing is to find out how time is actually being employed if such information is to assist in future work planning.

Naturally, most jobholders believe they have something more positive to contribute to the design of the job than the extent of their compliance with what has been prescribed. There will be some things that may be worth doing that have not been set out. Equally, time will have been spent on work that becomes attached to the job but which, in the estimation of the jobholder, contributes nothing of real value. That is where a careful distinction needs to be made between Grey and Pink Work. Both types of work lie outside the core area. The difference is that Grey Work is work that can reasonably be attached to the core area and is incidental to the job itself. Pink Work, on the other hand, has usually been grafted onto the job without supporting its main purpose. Pink Work is a sort of accretion that attaches itself to the body of work without being part of the system in the manner of a tumour. There comes a point when the jobholder is the first person to recognize that it needs to be removed. The jobholder may say 'What is the point of attending a meeting where I have nothing to say and no-one asks my opinion?' Not only is such an activity a waste of time but it stands in the way of getting on with the real job. Current systems hardly invite such a reaction.

So the feedback relates not only to the effect of changing demand on the work but to the way in which the jobholder perceives the work. One jobholder will perceive a superfluity of Pink Work; for another it will be small and reducing to a vanishing point. Just as in the case of any two people attending a meeting, one will view it as invaluable and another as merely an occupier of time space.

These different perceptions need to be brought to the surface. Denoting Pink Work can best be accomplished by choosing a suitable verb and attaching it to the appropriate colour so giving a formula that offers a face-saving way of putting over an unwelcome message. For example, the jobholder may choose the word 'attending' to convey presence at a meeting where time was spent to no good purpose. In contrast, another, engaged in the same meeting, might classify the activity as falling into the orange set and carry the verbs 'conferring' or 'collaborating'. Here the likelihood is that the item would already have been recorded by the original briefing and so would remain unaltered. Pink Work is a way in which jobholders can flag up warning signals.

Varying perceptions and varying aptitudes

In summary, the crux of the return message relates to the use of the colours grey, white and pink. These three colours cover different aspects of unspecified work. They are of significance in communicating how time is used outside the area of core work and how the jobholder perceives it. In effect, a large amount of Grey Work means 'I am spending a lot of my time on incidentals'. White Work says 'I think I am making a real contribution to improving things'. Pink Work announces 'A lot of my time is being wasted'. Helping the jobholder to make the appropriate selection of this colour trio, where non-core work is involved, should count as one of the most important functions of the effective facilitator.

Facilitators need to discriminate not only between types of work but also between jobholders with differing capabilities. Jobholders certainly respond differently to their briefings. In some companies wishing to put their best foot forward, the prospective jobholders chosen were a very able bunch, almost over-ready to make a personal contribution. For example, on one occasion our research worker was telephoned by an enthusiast for the pilot programme, keen to check that the jobholder return sheets were being filled in correctly and as desired. There were other occasions where minimal effort was made to complete or embellish the returns.

The most sophisticated jobholders were often keen to amend the core colour sheets along the lines they thought more appropriate. For example, in an early pilot trial one very proactive jobholder insisted on erasing a blue item and reworded it for entry on the yellow sheet. In effect, the jobholder would be saying 'I would prefer to tackle the job in this way'.

Nevertheless, there were arguments against allowing jobholders to make intervention along such lines; otherwise all procedures would be liable to fall into disarray. So henceforth they were not allowed to make any changes to the wording of the core work. Where they had not carried out the work exactly as stated, they would record a null time entry and then on the grey sheet would record the work in the way it had been carried out. The facilitator was then well placed to pass on the observations of the jobholder when the aggregate feedback data were presented to the manager. A submission for the reclassification of aspects of a job can always be considered by the manager to advantage. And it is at that point that managers can usefully talk to jobholders. In effect, the jobholder is saying to the manager 'Why don't you leave to to me how to go about it, because I think that will bring better results'. And the manager may say 'Yes, but on condition . . .'

A decision to sanction a proposed change along certain lines will mean that a bottom-up improvement has been brought about. The decision to reject the proposal implies that someone is approaching the job in a way that creates more difficulties than advantages. Here any resulting decision on the part of the manager to move the jobholder to different work offers a possible double benefit: the jobholder will now be engaged in work more suited to his or her propensities and can be replaced by someone who acts more in the style required. In the case of the sophisticated, the opportunities for open entries on pink and white sheets is inviting. Even more radical propositions can be put forward than those involving modifications in the disposition of work as between the four basic colours.

In the case of the less sophisticated, the object is to garner a view on how the work is seen without creating undue pressure. The method we developed for all jobholders involved less writing than in the first pilot trials and is especially apt for those less articulate than the average. The facilitator is there to help. He or she is then in a position to paraphrase useful points and to enter them appropriately on the grey, white and pink sheets. Here the facilitator provides a service to the

Jobholder and thereby improves communications between the job-holder and the manager.

The key personal quality of a facilitator is an understanding of people. That is never easy. What people say and what people mean can commonly be two different things. The initial assumption has to be that people mean what they say. But if fear or a shortage of suitable words gets in the way the facilitator needs to be there to help out. At any rate he or she is responsible for ensuring that only useful inputs are entered into the information system, for, in order to extract the fullest value, these have to be computerized against a background of the ever-present warning where computers are concerned: 'garbage in, garbage out.'

The greatest asset of a computer system is that it digests information and thrives on quantitative material. That permits immediate outputs that get right to the heart of the matter. In effect, by getting rid of the 'noise', the computer becomes a marvellous agent for improving communications.

Use of the colour sets proved to be helpful to communication at the oral level. But beyond that stage a new challenge beckoned which was to find a means to convert information that is normally passed orally into a numerical form so allowing it to be rapidly processed. Against that ambitious goal headway was made only slowly. But eventual progress enabled a significant step forward to be taken in the practical application of the theory of work sets: this is described in the next chapter.

8
Quantifying the way we work —

A readiness to communicate effectively with people at all levels is often considered the hallmark of the good manager. And yet this desirable condition is seldom to be observed in practice at the more senior reaches of management. The majority of employees feel they lack the benefits of face-to-face contact with those they believe to be the real wielders of power. And the resulting sense of alienation gives rise to numerous misunderstandings. Can it be that senior managers have ignored the importance of communications? I do not think that can be the explanation. Managers commonly talk about these matters and are always on the lookout for solutions. The problem arises from the fact that in the eyes of most employees communication is seen primarily as an oral activity. People like to talk about their work and they appreciate those who listen. But if such aspirations were to be generally met and managers were to communicate directly with all their employees, they would soon be awash in a sea of words. A vast load of other business awaiting attention on a manager's in-tray would die of neglect.

There has to be another way forward. Here a precedent has already been found on the economic front, for much of the to-ing and fro-ing of business communications lends itself to enumeration. A few figures can contain a vast amount of information. People exchange figures. They trade in estimates and actuals. They muse over figures before they make decisions. Many top managers are figure people to a supreme degree. Without figures they would be lost. Ten figures – from nought to nine in their various arrangements – constitute all that is, or ever has been, conveyed in numerical information.

The problem that needs to be addressed in this context is how employees can 'discuss' their work with managers and can do so in a form that, at least to begin with, can be cast in the familiar mould of figures. Were that aim to be accomplished, managers could afford the time to look more closely at work issues. Then there might be a prospect that all would benefit as a result.

The only likely way of accomplishing that aim lies in using the services of a professional (here termed the facilitator) who can compile, extract and process information about work so that it becomes the numerical input to a computer-based system from which it can then be converted back into words and charts (or graphical representation of the job). The effect is to allow a jobholder to 'talk' about the job, as he or she sees it, about what is wrong with it and about how it might be improved.

Although this may seem a highly contrived way of going about something simple, the main difference between computer-converted talking and real talking is that a filter device is protecting the manager from 'noise' talk. By looking at the numerical and graphical summaries the manager can see at a glance what appears interesting. A file can then be opened up and a form of talking begins. The out-of-the-ordinary is what arouses interest. That approach fits in with what is generally known as management by exception. If a decision is made, or contemplated, which affects the jobholder, the process is put into reverse. The redrafting of the job boundaries can be presented to the jobholder by the intermediary, the facilitator, so that a dialogue can begin. Alternatively, the manager can become a direct participant. In that case real 'talking' begins. These technical advances enable managers to retain a much closer grip on affairs in flatter organizations where there are fewer opportunities to keep in regular touch with ongoing work.

Processing the material

A number of early open-ended trials started with this end in view. But it soon became apparent that jobholders had considerable difficulty in providing one of the key numerical elements – an estimate of the time spent in each of the seven Workset colour categories. This difficulty was aggravated when jobholders had to wrestle with the meaning of the differences between the colour sets themselves. Some of these activities, although different in principle, were seen as too abstract to the jobholder to be distinguishable. So the exercise was soon aborted.

Eventually the problem of securing an estimate of time spent on the various colour-set activities was satisfactorily overcome by resorting to two measures. The first was that the basic responsibility for the breakdown of the job was transferred to the facilitator (acting in conjunction with the manager). The various components of the job were entered onto the appropriately coloured paper of the four core colour sets. There was therefore no overt necessity for the jobholder to wrestle with the meaning of the distinctions, so becoming sidetracked from assessing how time was spent.

The second measure was to simplify the treatment of time. As a first step, broad time periods were used against each of the items specified within a colour set. One advantage of the time period was that it reduced any sense of pressure to account precisely for all the time spent minute by minute during the day or reference period. However, as the ideal time period could vary from job to job, another more flexible means for recording time seemed to be needed. The next step was to introduce new units that we termed time keys. These could encompass different units of time on different jobs. That did not matter. What did matter was that relative time was recorded as between the seven colour sets. So after the four core colours had been dealt with, the three remaining colours were brought into the picture. The facilitator would then concentrate on finding, in collaboration with the jobholder, a form of words that gave adequate expression to the items to be entered on the grey, white and pink sheets and the time keys were employed in a similar way.

This method was essentially a compromise. We did not feel we could ask jobholders to account for the use of their time in any greater detail by, for example, keeping a time log, for to do so would have imposed on them an undue burden which they would doubtless have resisted. By employing the vaguer time keys we were saying 'We only want a rough idea for the purpose of work planning. We believe it is up to you to decide how time is best spent. After all, you are the one closest to the reality of the job.'

And yet something definite was required if the rank order of the manager's priorities were to be related mathematically to the reality of what was actually happening. Much depended on the exercise of priorities in the deployment of time by the person actually doing the job. So some figures were ultimately needed on the distribution of working time between each of the colour sets.

That compromise proved largely acceptable in practice. From entries on the time keys within the colour sets coupled with how time was used between the colour sets, the computer could offer a model on how the manager's view of the job differed from the jobholder's. In effect, the jobholder was communicating with the manager in a numerical way, saying something like 'Well, you asked me to give attention to 'this' and 'that'. 'This' has taken up much of my time but 'that' has not figured very much. However, I have managed to accomplish this other [specified] work but I have also been held back by certain other activities in which I have become embroiled that don't seem to me to serve much useful purpose.'

In reality, few workers would talk like that to their bosses even if the occasion presented itself. Close and intimate communication is prevented by a mutual expectation of status relationships and the boundaries defining what is considered a suitable topic for conversation.

The formula that offers a basis for closer communication ironically starts by making the parties more distant. By this means information is elicited in a more secure social environment and cast in a form, with the aid of the facilitator, which is unlikely to give offence. So in the end the two parties are able to communicate with one another more closely through the medium with which managers are commonly more comfortable – i.e. figures. The figures are, of course, rapidly turned back into words by the computer. A solid basis for discussion is then made possible. Indeed, experience suggests such discussion is more likely to happen after completing the preliminaries procedures of Workset because by then the two parties feel more confident that what they need to talk about will not be obstructed by formalities or held back by uncertainties. A secure starting point, acting as a guarantee against wasted time, facilitates productive conversation.

Individual differences expressed in figures

The traditional way of setting up a job requires that all specified work is carried out in a set way in the time allowed for each element. If that were to happen all workers, properly trained and instructed, would carry out their duties on any given job in like fashion and with broadly similar results.

However, my experience has taught me that workers will take advantage of every opportunity to depart from what has been laid down and to place their own particular stamp on how they carry out the job. That opportunity for individual expression is increased as 'jobs' lose their traditionally restricted character. Increasingly they come to refer to some agreed work domain encompassing a range of miscellaneous duties. A jobholder is thus able to pick and choose on the elements competing for attention without in any way departing from the briefing laid down. For managers to know what is going on is becoming difficult even under stable conditions, and it is becoming more difficult still as organizations become flatter and the span of perception becomes wider.

There has in the past been a dearth of information for ascertaining how a jobholder, or indeed any employee, carried out a job. But the introduction of quantification, even in its relatively crude form, pointed the way for discovering how individuals interpreted their assigned work in a behavioural sense.

Our pilot studies underlined the pronounced nature of individual differences. These assume a special significance where they depart from the expectations of the manager, which, of course, was available to us from the documentation of Workset.

Here two types of departure came to the fore. The first was a trend, especially evident in some graduates, to convert a work assignment into Yellow Work. Much of the briefing might be in Blue Work. But, however the job was set up, the result would be a heavy shading of yellow. In effect, the jobholder was saying: 'I'll do it my way'.

The second type of departure was the inflation of the green. Of all the patterns indicative of the discrepancy between how the job was set up and how it was actually carried out, this was the most conspicuous. The meaning is clear. Some people are saying, in a muted fashion, 'I find work satisfying when I can see and talk to people'. Of course, they would never dare express it as bluntly as that. The thought might not even occur to them consciously. But that is the message carried by their behaviour. Somehow, whatever they are asked to do gets converted into a form of socially engaging activity which still passes as, and contains many of the features of, work.

If this latter trend is as generally marked as it has appeared in our pilot studies in quantification, there is a general issue it raises. Should managers set up work in a way that recognizes the human need for social interaction? Or should the first priority be to establish the individual nature of the personal work pattern? A positive answer to either of these questions would call for a style of management quite different from that which generally holds today.

A query on the colour mix

From the viewpoint of the practical steps that can be taken by managers there remained one crunch question that arose out of analysis of the numbers and was connected with a matter of interpretation: are these figures exposing a phenomenon of real importance or are they not?

The query arose from the fact that the manager would brief the jobholder in the four core colours and receive in return feedback on how the job was progressing in seven colours. On examination of the feedback it was common to find that however the job had been set up in terms of the main colour set and its predominant claim on a jobholder's time, the jobholder had moved away from that particular emphasis. In other words, the jobholder would spend less than the time expected on that principal feature of the work.

A possible explanation was that with seven colours available for expressing the way in which time had been used, the jobholder was less likely to spend the expected time on the core colour sets as a group. After all, time was being redistributed from four starting sets to seven finishing sets. Yet I did not find that largely theoretical possibility convincing as an adequate explanation of what was really happening. The reason, simply, was that analysis showed that the extra three (non-core) colours were not generally using up a large amount of the available time. So the tendency to spend less time on the work the manager saw as the principal focus of the jobholder existed independently of the difference in circumstances in which the two perceptions were being made. It is a point that can be brought out and expressed in another way, to which a more positive interpretation may be attached. People like to vary their work and even if they are pressurized to spend too much time, as they see it, on one class of work, they will tend to move to another and will rationalize the reasons for so doing or, under current practices, will conceal the differences between what is specified by the manager and what they actually do.

The numerical feedback on how time is spent is therefore important for establishing whether the key work is being done or being neglected; it is important for finding out whether jobholders are being distracted by the call of other often less essential duties or even by interruptions that serve no useful purpose. Such feedback also serves a wider purpose in enabling a manager to understand an individual's personal style of working.

From our initial studies it appears that many employees share certain likes and dislikes in common. They are happy enough to perform a certain amount of prescribed work, but they will also look for an area in which they can exercise discretion and feel they have an element of personal responsibility. Similarly, they will be prepared to work alone for a while, but there will be a limit to their endurance and beyond a certain point they will find an excuse for working with others.

These patterns of working behaviour have a certain commonality. But overlying this common ground, such patterns can vary according to personal team roles, a point that will be examined further in Chapter 12. As human work becomes less closely supervised, there is even the prospect that such idiosyncratic tendencies will grow in magnitude until they reach the point where they thrust themselves onto the agenda of management.

A system of quantitative feedback, such as I have outlined in this chapter, allows one to come to terms with what is happening. New methods and techniques will help to improve an understanding of the psychology of work. The prize is something worth having. By tapping into the natural motivations of jobholders, jobs can be recast to make them more humanly acceptable and agreeable.

9

Managing the feedback ———

There is commonly a difference between the expectations of the manager about what a job is intended to deliver and the experience and perceptions of the jobholder about how the job is actually progressing. Such a difference could be a source of tension. But, properly handled, it can become a strength. That is why the preparation of the feedback is so important. The returning information has to be cast in a form that makes for ease of interpretation. Here the facilitator has a vital role to play in working to improve and maintain the reliability and quality of the information that is being processed.

It was something of a revelation to discover in pilot trials how little some managers knew about the nature of the work carried out by those reporting to them. For example, in one hospital study a declaration was made: 'My boss has no idea what I do.' In that context the comment was understandable. Hospitals are full of trained professionals. A boss is one type of professional while those accountable to that person belong to a different medical category. In these cases senior professionals are reluctant to see themselves as managers. They act with considerable authority without being truly managerial. That shortcoming meant that resources were wasted through not being properly deployed. Here the feedback helped to develop some senior professionals into a fuller managerial role.

In other instances there are those who see themselves as managers and are sure they know what is going on. Here the feedback fulfils a different purpose. There is now a cue for action springing from any observed discrepancies between what was expected and what was found to happen. Expressed simply, the manager reflects: 'Why isn't the jobholder doing the job as laid down? Why is the jobholder engaged in other activities that lie beyond the briefing?'

In general, there tend to be two contrasting answers. The first can imply that the jobholder is not up to the job or has misunderstood what was required. The second possibility is that the jobholder possesses such good sense that obsolete work items are being set aside in favour of activities that add greater value to the work that has been set.

There is a vast difference between these two positions. And yet the outward signs can be difficult to distinguish: it is how they are perceived and reacted to that matters most. One manager will be irritated that the job is not being carried out as prescribed, whereas another, when presented with the same information, will take the view that the person in the job is showing initiative and promise.

There is no absolute way of determining which is the correct judgement, for much depends on how a job has been cast in the first place and on the choice of employees to occupy that job. Clearly, some jobholders suit the style of certain managers and others not. By the same reckoning a group of employees could well decide that they would work better if they were made accountable to another manager. The whole process of putting together a group of people in a single socio-economic endeavour is an intricate business. Where so much can go wrong an interim goal is required. Here the objective is to provide the sort of information that in the long term will facilitate the emergence of a combination of people best suited to achieve a particular result.

Omissions, neglect and work-shift

The strength of the approach revolves round the method. The first step in the analysis of the feedback is to compare the use of time as envisaged by the manager with what is recorded by the jobholder. The manager's estimate is not communicated to the jobholder, for to do so would be to invite the jobholder to respond passively and unthinkingly to whatever was being demanded. Rather the need is to encourage local initiative and to focus on how the job is working out in reality.

A few work items on the jobholder brief may not be covered at all and thus have a zero entry recorded on the time key. Other items will show an estimate of the occupancy of time falling well below the amount the manager envisaged when the job was set up. Whether such evident underscoring suggests a problem or not depends partly on the colour set. On the blue items it would raise serious questions about whether standards are slipping with well-defined practices and procedures being disregarded. Some individuals are prone to neglect work aspects that need disciplined application, preferring to spend their time on socially attractive activities that bear only a superficial relationship to work, or becoming unduly sidetracked into Grey Work. For example, periodic calibration of equipment, itself a good example of Blue Work, demands a concentrated routine that would appear to offer no immediate reward and is less appealing than other work activities that compete for attention. Yet if such work is ignored or forgotten about, there can be serious consequences, as in hospitals where faulty measurement readings contribute to errors in diagnosis and treatment. Where a jobholder is found to neglect important Blue Work, the implication is that the jobholder is in the wrong job and would be better placed elsewhere. In other circumstances the omission of Blue Work may have a rational explanation. In the business world it is not uncommon to find that the need to be responsive to customers is paramount to meeting formal specifications. So here the Blue declines in favour of the Green. Whenever any major change in working habits is observed, further investigation will be called for. For example, it may be necessary to examine whether any significant shift in the pattern of orders or services has arisen.

Shortfalls in Green and Orange Work are seldom to be accounted for by a change in business or service circumstances. The more usual explanation revolves round the way people behave or prefer to behave. Some jobholders avoid work that has social dimensions, or are bothered by what they see as social pressures. Shy or socially maladroit people are often more comfortable when engaged in tasks that lie predominantly or even exclusively within their personal control. Here the implication is that they are less suited than others to Green and Orange Work.

A deficiency in Yellow Work may sometimes reflect a change in working demands but, so far, we have seen few instances of this. The more usual explanation is that personal factors are operating; or, put more simply, the jobholder is disinclined to shoulder responsibility and looks for support elsewhere, in which case there will be an expansion on the time estimates of Green and Orange Work.

The perceived gap that separates what a jobholder is supposed to be doing from what he or she is actually doing always raises the question of whether the person is a misfit in the job or is an active force in helping the job to progress. I can think of several cases of executives who have risen to eminence through disregarding the terms of their mandate, so both antagonizing their superiors and succeeding in justifying their precipitate actions at a single stroke. Whether on balance such unruly conduct proves an advantage is a debatable point. These are the very issues that often figure strongly in boardroom rows.

The general point is that where a jobholder is not performing a job in the way construed when it was first set up, the matter needs to be discussed rather than passed over. Under current practice this hardly happens. Since the process for highlighting such differences and getting them on the discussion agenda has been lacking, important issues have been largely ignored. Workers continue to engage in work that is unnecessary and a monument to the past; and at the same time they risk neglecting points of detail and application crucial to health and safety. Situations such as these need to be brought to the fore and exposed. But before that can happen, a closer look needs to be taken at the nature of the extra and unforeseen work that is being detected by analysis of the data.

The rise in unexpected work

In booming mass-production industries work largely corresponds with what is planned. In other industries and conditions no two days may be the same. Even in the manufacturing industry, while routine work is taken for granted, it does not necessarily dominate the scene because there are always new issues that are presenting themselves for attention. Here the jobholder has a valuable role to play in providing relevant information.

Once the jobholder has responded to the use of the time key according to the four core colour starting items, the facilitator asks 'What other work have you been doing?' It is surprising how readily and quickly people respond to the question and can nominate activities that have been left out of account.

Here the facilitator has two immediate duties. The first is to extract as much relevant material as possible for the given reference period. The second is to classify it. For each item the question to be asked internally is 'Should this be treated as grey, white or pink?'

If the item seems to belong essentially to the core work, but is merely a variant or expressed in the jobholder's preferred wording, the explanation is probably that the jobholder is trying to find an obliging answer to the question and has nothing significant to add to what has been covered before. Yet, in the main, jobholders do have something to add and they often do so with some evident gusto. This occurs especially where things have gone wrong. There have been mishaps, contingencies and interruptions. That is the very information that provides the feedstuff for future planning.

The focus in classification now falls on how the jobholder has reacted to these events. Certain sideshoots from the main stem of the work expand so as to take up increasing amounts of time until they can legitimately be counted as forms of additional work in their own right that have not hitherto been recognized. Such items can and should be classified as Grey Work: they are part of the unavoidable clutter that comes with every job and with which any reasonable employee should be able to cope without further question.

There is often other work that would seem related, but after further analysis and consideration turns out to be non-essential and unproductive. It contributes nothing: it is better classed as Pink Work. That is the value put on it by the facilitator. But from the point of view of the jobholder, the duty to act in that way is seen as essential. For example, waiting to see a boss who is engaged in a long telephone call in order to extract a signature on a document that has to be sent off urgently: that is a required activity in the eyes of the jobholder. On the other hand, the facilitator sees this as ineffective waiting time and possibly to be recorded as pink. Here he or she may explain the basic difference between Grey and Pink Work in a manner that makes it easier to arrive at the correct classification.

Differentiation between grey and pink can be difficult in some cases. But White Work, in contrast, stands out more clearly and is less subject to any possible confusion. The reason is that such work has been entered into proactively whereas the grey and the pink are more akin to reflex reactions to events and contingencies.

We found that virtually all managers were interested in the feedback on how the work was being tackled by those reporting to them. The differentiating factor, however, lay between those who merely said 'Oh, ah, how interesting' and those who were intent on acting on the information.

The action that prompted most constructive attention was the Pink Work and how it could be eliminated or reduced. Some jobholders are reluctant to report Pink Work fearing to 'sign their own death warrant'. In such cases it is better for the facilitator to approach the subject gradually and with sensitivity. 'Do you feel that this part of the job serves no useful purpose?'

The Pink Work associated with others is more readily observed and is less threatening. Once its existence is recognized, it can lead on to consideration of the Pink Work associated with the self. For example, managers in large organizations who are alerted to the issues and who seem to be forever 'in conference' have been quick to see the significance for themselves and to identify those meetings among the many that are notable for their pinkness. 'We could cut that one out for a start.'

In reality, meetings are seldom totally pink, for they generally have an ostensible and credible purpose from which all too often they are inclined to drift. A failure to establish a tight agenda and to stick to the agreed business is what beckons in the pink.

Examination of a growing body of Grey Work excites less attention and usually demands more active energy and consideration. Grey Work is less evidently a time waster but can act as a drag on the whole system. More specifically, it raises the question of whether it is sensible for someone with valued professional or technical skills to spend time on activities that could be done by others. Key personnel, now shorn of support by secretaries and assistants as part of an economy drive, spend their time making travel arrangements, providing tea and coffee for guests, sending faxes to deal with delays from suppliers or administrative mistakes in contracts and other miscellaneous matters. No-one has established whether, on balance, the alleged savings in ancillary support has resulted in an overall gain. The reason is simply that there has hitherto been no adequate means of examining and evaluating how work previously conducted has been redistributed and to what effect. Savings on the wages bill can be accomplished at the cost of allowing the personal productivity of key players to drop. Since that productivity is becoming increasingly difficult to measure in any clearly meaningful way, the reality of what goes on tends to be hidden from view. Savings have been accomplished in the areas that matter least. One is back to the adage that action is only taken on what is visible and measurable and the rest is ignored. Like an iceberg, it is what is under the water that counts. Meanwhile it is the ice above the water that attracts more and more precise measurement from the technocrats appointed to take charge of efficiency and it is they rather than the managers themselves who are now playing the tune.

Feedback on the white prompts what are probably the most fundamental questions. Is the innovation that has made its undaunted and uninvited entry into the job a welcome guest or should it be shown the door? Initiatives on the part of jobholders cannot be permitted without accepting an element of risk. The manager has to decide, usually in consultation with others and certainly with the jobholder, on the advisability of allowing the new element of work to continue. If it does, should that work be incorporated into the job as it is now or should it be recast for the jobholder? In the latter case it will no longer be White Work, but may become Yellow Work. Yet another possibility is that it should be reassigned to another where it could well take the form of Blue Work. It can also happen that a seemingly good idea falls short of its initial promise because it trespasses into the field of someone who is busy tackling the matter from another angle. The jobholder is unaware, so that an enterprising initiative ultimately produces no overall gain. Still, the enterprise of the jobholder has been noted by the manager and will be taken into consideration when new work is reassigned.

These are the issues with which managers must wrestle. And the process can start only when this new source of information becomes available.

10

Creating a new culture ─────────

To what extent does the means of setting up work influence the culture of the workplace? To the best of my belief that question has never been adequately addressed before. The significance of an answer in the affirmative to the question posed is that it would provide a new opening: an appropriate strategy could help in the development of a dynamic culture at the workplace. As it is, most executives who show interest in culture treat it as some fixed pattern of social traits beyond the reach of influence. Here culture is considered to present an often unwelcome challenge to which some response must be found.

The current interest in industrial culture owes much to the increased scale of transnational business operations. The discovery that as you cross frontiers workers and executives behave and express themselves in unexpected ways can lead to all manner of complications. Here cultural differences claiming attention fall into two distinctive categories.

The first relates to overt behaviours infrequently encountered in everyday settings and which strike the untravelled as strange on that account. Take the occasions when people meet, as occurs when new business relationships are entered into. Turks and Arabs will serve endless cups of tea and refrain from talking business. Slav business-men may kiss, Germans will shake hands on repeated occasions, Americans may administer a slap on the back. People stand somewhat closer to me in some countries than I would expect in England where any behaviour suggestive of physical proximity can have other meanings. In Denmark it is often the case that no progress can be expected until people share a laugh together. In Japan once the bowing has stopped, the formalities begin and it would be rash to draw any conclusion from whatever behaviour is to be observed. In Australia I expect to receive a derogatory comment about England, usually relating to its sporting failures, to which I will respond with some mocking comment about Australia; and a friendly relationship will be instantly set up. I would not care to try out that formula in other countries.

The matter of language

A second category of cultural difference covers words, phrases and language in general. An expression that counts as directness in one country will give offence in another. Nuances in verbal expressions are very important in French and English: the diplomatic conveyance of the most delicate message becomes possible, provided the words are chosen with precision. Conversely, such precision is lost when two people do not share a common first language and the door to misunderstanding is opened.

Inevitably culture is closely linked with language and when one language needs to be interpreted into another, special problems arise. If the interpreter makes a literal interpretation, an unsuitable turn of phrase may result and there will scarcely be time to adapt it culturally. Embarrassed interpreters have been heard to comment 'I don't think that would be a very wise thing to say'. Smaller linguistic groups have an understandable preference for a standard language which is plain in expression and from which subtle meanings and verbal etiquette can be largely excluded. With its absence of masculine and feminine nouns, and of adjectival forms that must agree with them, English confers a distinct advantage in reducing the load on memory for the new learner. Gender-free language also confers a now-favoured social advantage in the modern world, for its non-sexist nature has a psychic effect in encouraging the emancipation of women in areas that were once the preserve of men. On the basis of a world headcount, English may not be as widely spoken as Mandarin but its strength lies in its widely adopted use as a cross-cultural second language, the standard means of communicating in business and in flying, and a contributor to some measure of common understanding wherever strangers meet and struggle for words.

English owed its spread in the first place to the British Empire, on which the sun never set; yet, when the Empire withered, a legacy of language was left behind that served as a reconciler between different linguistic groups whose own language could pose the risk of dominance in transactions between them.

The next step in the global spread of English came through the rising economic power of North America. The United States, and its neighbour Canada, constitutes the largest economic region in the world. The world craves for American investment as the short road to prosperity. Language comes as part of the package. North America has had perhaps the most successful record in the world for absorbing large numbers of immigrants and creating the conditions in which different peoples could live peacefully alongside each other. Yet, outside English-speaking countries, the United States itself has a poor record in coping with cultural matters in its overseas investments. That is not the contradiction it may sound. The focus of America has been on assimilating immigrants, with the Statue of Liberty holding out its symbolic torch to welcome arrivals from foreign lands to freedom, enlightenment and the fruits of American citizenship. Adherence to traditional culture was a force operating counter to Americanization. That lesson was consolidated and when Americans established businesses overseas, they preferred to take with them their own language and culture.

There are undoubted advantages in the use of a common language to overcome communication and cultural barriers and English is currently performing that function. And yet there is a negative side. Any imposed language risks being treated as some vestige of imperialism operating against the sense of community: it may encourage sub-cultures to develop that can strive for their own reference points and independence. For centuries Poland was overrun in oscillating waves by Swedes, Russians, Austrians and Germans. Yet the Polish language remains remarkably free of foreign words which were fended off by Polish spirit. Language and culture lose their vitality when borrowed; their vigour depends on a continued growth.

Allowing a culture to develop

If managers are to adopt and encourage a proactive approach to culture, a new starting point is needed. That point should be the workplace itself. The most fertile location for real cultural growth is the meeting place for immigrant workers who rush to avail themselves of work opportunities when the consequence of a shortage of labour has been the removal of immigration barriers. The effect is to bring about on particular sites an assembly of workers who may have difficulty in communicating with one another. Drawn from no common background they share no common purpose other than to earn a living. In the past the only bonds that united them were those that gave them common cause against an employer, which depended on grievances about working conditions and which sprang from fears for their future.

Such a setting does, however, present a positive opportunity. The demands of work create social relationships which in the first place have to be functional. Here language is not only important but also essential. For example, Swahili and Pidgin were originally artificial creations, intentionally developed as a linguistic compromise to allow those speaking unrelated languages to communicate for purposes of work and trade. Their vocabularies then grew naturally, acquiring a momentum of their own. Ultimately, as living languages they generated their own culture.

Given time, all workplaces tend to develop a local language connected with the jargon of whatever technology is being used. There is an official jargon and sometimes an unofficial, shopfloor-bred, jargon. The latter, especially, serves to create intimate bonds of communication, just as happens in the use of Cockney rhyming slang.

I was first struck by the opportunities that occur when a new language can be introduced by my experiences with team-role terminology. As a result of earlier research, consolidated by a great deal of subsequent industrial application, I had isolated nine distinctive team roles in terms of which the contributions of team members could be described. In due course the theory of team roles and the use of the computer-based Human Resource Management System, Interplace, that accompanied it became widely used in many parts of the world and led to my visits to many countries. The ideas and the method were directed in the first place for use in management teams and project teams. I would maintain that the target population were executives on the grounds that their jobs were less structured and so provided the conditions under which discretion could be used in deciding how to behave in interpersonal working relationships. That is why, when asked, I felt the need to admit that the approach was not suitable in connection with blue-collar jobs where such discretion was seldom permissible.

But on two occasions users of the system, who were independent training consultants, insisted that I was wrong and that there were places where the concepts of team roles had been particularly well received by blue-collar workers. Both instances, however, though far apart geographically, had a notable link. One was located in a construction site in a Gulf State and the other in a wine-making business in South Australia. The link was that both sites employed a high proportion of immigrants from a wide range of countries. Inevitably there was a language problem. The consultants had been engaged to weld the workers into an effective working group. Here the concept of team roles provided a looked-for solution. Part of the reason appeared to have been that the workers had to learn only nine concepts. Once grasped, the concepts themselves could be used and manipulated through their own mother tongues and English could be bypassed. The workers began to talk among themselves in these terms. The growth of a site culture had been given a fillip by the importation of a jargon language. Here culture almost bears comparison with the use of the same word that has an unrelated meaning – the starter yeast cultures used in wineries. On that analogy, once a starter is used, a process begins, resulting in rapid fermentation. It is a similar social fermentation that the wise manager should try to encourage.

Cultures in the making: cultures adapting

The earliest recorded human art comes down to us in the form of cave paintings in scenes typically depicting animals usually festooned by an assortment of spears and arrows. Hunters were celebrating the chase and grafting onto it deeper meanings. Around this activity, and deep in the cave, experts surmise there grew up cults with a dynamic role that played a pivotal role in each society. Work and sport must have been indistinguishable as unified forms of human activity, linked by particular sets of beliefs about the world and by relationships between the hunters.

In a modern industrial society, work and sport, so far from being integrated with one another, stand in evident contrast. In most engineering firms the walls of the typical machine shop will be adorned with nude women and football stars. Such pictures are escapist: they are unconnected with the work itself. Work and sport are like estranged neighbours who live side by side but never mix. Thinking, too, is fenced in by the work environment and offers no adequate outlet. Cerebration ticks over at a minimum level of energy consumption, rising in its energy output only for the placing of bets in types of gambling that are bereft of true action control. It is understandable therefore that the culture of the workplace fails as a culture creator: it is the passive recipient of whatever exists outside the workplace.

Where people enjoy some greater measure of control over their working lives, cultural forms spring more readily from the workplace. The cult of freemasonary sprang from self-employed builders and spread into other professions. What it was able to generate was the advantages of preferential business treatment encased in its rich cult of mystique and rituals. So too where the hazards of mining create the conditions for the close bonding of miners, a real culture develops in trade unionism. The miners cannot adorn the walls of the mine with cave paintings in the manner of their ancient forebears, for the coal that forms the walls has to be extracted. But the culture of these cave-dwellers literally surfaces in open-air events, offering rich pageantry and tradition, as in the Durham Miners Gala.

The decline in labour-intensive coal mining has discharged into the community large numbers of miners in search of other jobs. Some of these have taken with them, whether subconsciously or not, many of the attributes of a coal-mining culture. During the writing of this chapter chance had it that I was engaged as a judge in the annual award of the Top Team for Public Sector Work in the United Kingdom. There were forty entries, covering all manner of activities from police work to social security administration. These entries were narrowed to a short list of four who were then required to make a public presentation of their case and to submit to team questioning. The eventual winner, by a unanimous decision of the judges, was the garbage-collecting service of Mansfield District Council. The dustmen of this council had hitherto had offered a poor service and had showed many signs of surly and uncooperative behaviour. About 30 per cent of their number were gradually replaced by ex-miners. While it may be difficult to establish any primary cause on how it came about that a deficient service became transformed into a national award winner, the change in the composition of the workforce cannot be without significance. Miners are renowned for their readiness to help one another. A closely knit body of men develop bonds in cooperative behaviour that with appropriate encouragement can be transferred to other situations.

Outside certain industries where hazardous conditions prevail, the denizens of the average workplace have been largely drained of energy and inspiration by modern industrial processes. Whatever patterns of activities and professed values are to be found have been imposed by the bosses. Statements of values now arrive in the form of written memos, which it is the duty of training officers to impart to the workers with the help of exercises and briefings. Even environmental improvement in the workplace is brought about by imposition rather than through a cultural process. The open plan of the large office may contain many commendable features and yet earn as much disapproval as approval. Often it is not the result so much as the process leading to a result that matters most in the end.

Yet there are signs of a certain cultural revitalization. Team empowerment has enabled small groups of workers in some manufacturing establishments to decorate their own surroundings. That is how pot plants are to be seen flourishing incongruously in some corner of an otherwise bleak factory. In this instance there is no comparison with the open-plan landscaped office which may have greater artistic unity but is devoid of the human touch.

Putting colour into culture

Words and language are the very material out of which culture is built and, in the case of material culture, its forerunners. And yet in a multi-ethnic, multi-lingual society words become hurdles and often need to be supplemented by other means of communication, like gesture. Resort to more primitive modes of communication increases the capacity for conveying meaning. Yet the ambiguities arising out of gesture dilute its advantage and can put mutual understanding at risk.

Colour is, in contrast, a modality well suited to universal perception regardless of the beholder. The message that colour conveys will be the same for all regardless of social background, being subject to distortion only through the rarer conditions of ocular dysfunction. Colour offers itself as a simple language and communication code, facilitating exchanges between people who are culturally dissimilar. Such a language, being work-related, can overcome the polyglot complications of the workplace and offer a common basis for the emergence of new cultural forms.

I have observed that people are quick to adopt the language in jest. A person who is engaged in an activity leading nowhere will be said to be conducting Pink Work. A fellow-worker in a jocular counter-accusation will reply that it is a long time since the observer ever did any Blue Work. Someone busy with an activity unrelated to current demands and priorities will excuse this neglect on grounds of undertaking White Work.

The language of this colour code has a small vocabulary. Yet its add-on value is large because it extends the meaning of whatever language is already there. Most recognized languages of the world extend infinitely back into time, vanishing into the mists of antiquity in a way that is difficult to trace. By contrast, there are a few more local and vernacular languages whose birth has been witnessed in the modern era. They have sprung from work and commerce. They have been consolidated where social stability and cohesion have followed from some continuing measure of successful economic activity.

Improved ways of working that offer long-term stability in combination with the stimulus of new challenges and experiences offer a seedbed from which the new shoots of culture can spring to life.

11

Fostering team empowerment —————————————

Expressed in accordance with the jargon of this book and given the appropriate culture in which devolution can flourish at the workplace, team empowerment denotes Orange Work. Yet that conclusion hardly constitutes a significant step forward. If a group of people are given responsibility for all the work they agree to undertake, they still have to determine how that work is to be divided among themselves. Sadly, it is a common experience that this transfer can make their jobs more difficult than formerly. The problem, usually unforeseen by the advocates of team empowerment, is that unless there is a naturally occurring and acceptable distribution of duties, often requiring a fully compatible group of work associates, there is no established mechanism for deciding who does what. A lack of direction and order can soon become apparent. At least under traditional arrangements the manager is always present to act as the arbiter or the decision maker. He or she still remains, of course, a resource to which the empowered group could refer in the event of a failure to progress as well as desired. In principle, they could always say:

> We are grateful for your faith in us and for the responsibility we have been given. But we can't decide ourselves how the work should be spread. Could you help us?

Such an admission is very unlikely to take place. Just as individuals seek to save face, groups do too. With human nature being as it is, the more likely outcome, following disagreement or indecision, is that the group will cover up any shortcomings and place the blame on some third party; and because the usual monitoring processes employed by management are lacking, it will be some time before the group is exposed. And when that ultimately happens, it is a near-certainty that team empowerment will be abandoned.

The only condition where team empowerment stands a fair chance of working and surviving in the long term is where team members are given the same information as is available to managers. That lesson is well established in respect of financial and business information, for there are a few instances (though not many) where groups of well-informed workers have managed their own units remarkably well without the need for supervision and external direction. The question is whether that theorem about the critical utility of information applies equally to the patterning of tasks and responsibilities. Can this crucial information be routed directly to team members other than through the agency of the manager?

I confess that I had originally thought that without the manager acting as a pivot there would be no clear way of sorting out the jumble. There is always the risk of acrimony and resentment shown towards any interventionist, even within the group, who takes a stand on what should be done without the backing of authority. However, I have had to revise my views somewhat in the light of recent experience.

A case of horizontal accountability

A general principle of good organization is that everyone should be accountable to someone, or to some supervisory body at least, for otherwise the system in which people are embroiled in work risks abuse. In other words, there is a strong case for adhering to a form of vertical accountability.

Certainly, large-scale human organizations have to start that way. The issue is whether, once started, that pattern should continue unmodified. The pilot studies we conducted in introducing Workset into a hospital began in the way we had conceived at the start. Members of a clinic had their jobs set out in the core colours and in a fitting language by the managers to whom the jobholders were accountable and the information about how the job was being actually performed was duly fed back in the seven colours of Workset along with their time allocations. Thereafter there was a buzz of excitement as a result of certain facts being revealed for the very first time. managers and jobholders met to discuss the discrepancies and their implications. What especially engaged attention was that different people could interpret what was supposedly the same job in such different ways. This would not be a surprise where people worked alongside one another as in an active collaborative team and different ways of working were open to observation. But the message was sharper and raised more searching questions where they were engaged on the same job but on different shifts and so would not encounter each other except at change-over.

People love to talk about their jobs, although few are prepared to show much interest in a job of which they have no personal knowledge and experience. So talkers go in search of listeners and they duly find them among their close colleagues where they can swap stories and views. In our hospital environment an upward-reporting system soon changed its character and resulted in a closely knit group of co-workers pressing their manager to arrange for staff to confer. In other words, there was a move to bypass the manager.

And so lateral meetings were held. And the next stage was that the identification of anomalies in working practice and the recognition of omissions could be sorted out by the jobholders themselves. This shifted the role of the manager in the direction of becoming an agent. This outward-facing agent would then act on behalf of the team in order to reduce those constraints and pressures which the jobholders themselves could not address and which impinged on their ability to deliver a fully professional service. In return the jobholders would rearrange the disposition of their own duties where that did not necessitate the intervention of the manager.

This type of advanced horizontal accountabililty can result in spontaneous changes that affect the distribution and incidence of Blue, Green, Yellow, White and Pink Work (in this last case leading to its reduction). So the acceptance of Orange Work can have a dynamic effect on these other colours. The crucial question is whether horizontal accountability can come about of its own accord or whether it can only be set up as a secondary activity through an appropriate form of vertical accountability.

I have asked myself this question without being entirely sure of the answer. It could be that the one type of accountability does not need the other provided the team is well balanced and in receipt of all the requisite information that Workset normally feeds to the manager. On the other hand, I have to admit that the only exemplary cases I have witnessed of horizontal accountability have occurred in the domain of exemplary managers. There is something paradoxical about that. If an exemplary case places less reliance on the manager, why does it need an exemplary manager to set it up?

Here I can hazard a guess. In the first place the manager takes the lead in setting up the process. 'This job is not being done as required. This person is overloaded, that person is underloaded. An undue amount of Pink Work in this area can be cut out if we take such-and-such action.' But then it occurs to the team that they could make the same adjustments as the manager might demand given the same information. Make them accountable for the results and it will happen. It may even happen more efficiently than before because the members of the team are on the spot and the manager isn't. And so the team develops a new orientation which involves reporting to one another. That is the second stage and is the essence of horizontal accountability.

Training the team

Team empowerment can be a rewarding form of organization if only it works. A prime requirement is that members understand each other. Team roles and their exchange between team members have often been used to advantage in research and development and project teams. But where manual workers are concerned their use has been more restricted. That is because the focus of work falls more on tasks than on establishing roles and forging role relationships. An additional difficulty is that the language of team roles with their closely defined character does not make for easy assimilation by those with a limited education. But this is less of a problem with the colour language of Workset. The concepts themselves are easier to put across, for they hinge on only four types of work demand. Even so, we have learned that where manual workers are concerned it can be a mistake to start with the concepts themselves, as though approaching the issues are rooted in some arcane philosophical or metaphysical standpoint. Any such suspicion would cast doubt on its practical value. Better to aim at a low-profile change in procedures. Differences in urgencies and demands are seen to be represented on different coloured sheets. Blue is urgent in the sense that the work has to be done in a very particular way. Green is less urgent but does mean that common sense is needed in the way you carry it out. Yellow means that you alone are accountable for the results, while orange signifies that you share that responsibility with others.

That is all that is needed in explanation. The colour language needs time in order to establish itself in the group. It now becomes an open question whether a facilitator should work with the group and use the full seven-colour feedback system. Where the jobs have stabilized there is a case for not doing so, for development of the job is not seen as one of the prime objectives. The alternative is that the manager works initially with the group assigning the colours along with the appropriate content to the individuals and allows the situation to evolve. In due course a moment will arrive when the best distribution has been reached and the system is accepted.

Then the manager can say to the group: 'Well, we've now reached the stage when we can make you collectively responsible for what you achieve in the ABC Unit. Sort out the work among yourselves as best you can.'

So by such an enabling procedure the group turns into an empowered team. The manager is still in charge in principle. But his or her approach should be limited to 'management by exception'. Horizontal accountability now takes over much of the work that would normally occupy the manager. From now on, the team endeavours to maintain an equitable balance in the way in which work is distributed.

There is a lot that can go wrong on this road to the devolution of responsibility: the culture of the organization may prejudice the prospects for successful innovation; the manager may fail to carry the message convincingly; the people who form the team may be ill-sorted. In the case of our hospital environment we had one cultural advantage in that in the field of health the principle of interdisciplinary teams is widely accepted. Certainly there is much to be gained if the goal of getting people to work togther without reliance on authority can be accomplished. After all, co-workers are on the spot when decisions need to be made. They can take immediate action and need no longer suffer the delay of 'waiting for the manager'.

A general point worth stressing is that if team empowerment is to be made viable it needs to be more than a free-floating arrangement: it should come about through a sequence of initiatives and should create its own informal structure. Without any structure a group is no more than a melee.

My conclusion is that there is no contradiction between horizontal and vertical accountability. Admittedly, with more of the one you need less of the other. And yet there is a certain interdependence. The right type of vertical responsibility creates the conditions in which horizontal accountability can flourish.

There is an analogy here between groups and their mega-cousins, national states. A fully autonomous group in a business organization can create chaos. So also, a state that waves the flag of nationalism and operates solely in what it hails as its own national interests creates crisis in the world community, the very condition that has preceded most wars. Yet nationalism is not contradicted by the recognition of a supranational authority. Indeed, it is the only condition in which nationalism can operate without damage to itself and others in the modern world.

In terms of groups and social relationships one needs to begin at the beginning. The group cannot be set up in the abstract as though it had no reference to any other body. Its external relationships affect its internal functioning. The relationships between the various groups form the lynchpin of the body politic. That is why, if we succeed in making the empowered team a viable organization that can stand the test of time, we are creating those more stable building blocks on which a larger social edifice can ultimately rest.

12

From competence to excellence ————————

The language for describing work has a momentous influence on the way in which work is approached because the values it embodies translate into attitudes. Duty, application, conscientiousness have helped to embody the Protestant work ethic. But such words lose specific utility when it comes to differentiation between the various types of work that make up a complex set of industrial operations.

The early Industrial Revolution boosted the emergence of a new and finely fashioned language of work. Borrowing from the guilds, it was based on trades – trades which were given formal recognition and involved time-served apprenticeships. If that revolution had consolidated a set of unchanging basic work patterns, no further problem would have arisen. But industry moves on. New operations were born that could no longer fit into the old classification. It must have been an epoch-making event in industrial history when management first acknowledged that a few men knew the exact moment when a furnace was best tapped: they had developed valuable skills on their own account. In their own mysterious way, some workers managed to achieve output targets and quality, while bypassing whatever traditional teachings of apprenticeship were around.

A new language was needed to describe this challenging phenomenon and its centrepiece was Skill. Some workers possessed skills which others envied but would fail to reach, so allowing the skilled worker to retain a secure grip on the job allied, very often, with high personal earnings.

Individual differences in aptitude and the ability to acquire or develop arcane techniques could account for much of the variation in labour productivity. The lesson at last got home to management. If the general level of productivity was to be raised, the skilled worker would need to be studied. So Skills Analysis was born.

The experts who were brought in to pioneer these studies came from an academic background, with psychologists eminent in the study of psychomotor skills playing a leading role. Consequent on close connection with operational experience, a theory of skill came into being. Douglas Seymour's *Industrial Training for Manual Operations* (Pitman, 1954) became the classic work of the period. White-collar experts were soon studying blue-collar experts to see how they did it.

Skills versus standards

A crude classification of industrial work could now produce the following – skilled work was what a few workers could do, semi-skilled work was what was possible after some training and unskilled work was what every worker could do. The work study experts would set out to overcome costly production bottlenecks by reducing the volume of skilled work, and consequentially increasing the amount of semi-skilled work. New training programmes were designed to make skilled work more accessible to others, thereby effectively lowering its skill level.

This classification of work and its relationship to pay, whatever its merits, was basically unstable. An engine was created for eroding the system by diluting skill. Workers soon became suspicious of management's intentions. Improvements designed to speed production and progress fell short of their potential as much of the ground gained was lost through industrial strife.

Classifying work in terms of skills placed an emphasis on the domestic processes of how to get there rather than on the output itself. The world, however, was becoming client-oriented and market-driven. The focus was fast changing in an external direction towards quality. And quality dealt in standards. While skills tended to vary due to all sorts of factors including individual aptitudes, standards were tangible. Standards lent themselves to being defined in terms of client needs or, failing that, through the technical recommendations of bodies representing particular trades and industries.

Once the criteria were established, a product was up to standard or not up to standard. Industry now began to draw the collective gaze of its employees outwards towards its customers instead of inwardly towards its skill and pay differentials, which were often divisive issues of little concern to the world outside.

Suddenly a great race started to establish standards. National committees proliferated in all sectors of the economy. Companies, that had won recognition for meeting whatever standards had been laid down, waved their approval certificates as publicly as possible. A new era of Quality appeared to have begun.

In terms of the colour classification of work, the focus on specified standards as a guide to management in its approach to employees and to jobs could have but one obvious consequence. There was a growth in Blue Work. Blue Work was a means of proving to others, especially inspectors, that the company was up to standard. Blue Work had become *de rigueur* and its reach spread so far as to colour the Management Charter Initiative itself. Blue Work now tightened its grip not only on blue-collar workers but on the managers too. They had to reach specified standards of behaviour and accomplishment. These were known as competencies. The language of skills was dropped and the language of competencies took its place. In my periodic trips round the world I could not fail to notice that after what seemed a short interval, in which competencies carried no particular message, the term had entered into the everyday vocabulary of management on opposite sides of the world. So fast did this spread occur that I was reminded of the march of the triffids. Did all these managers mean the same thing by the occurrence that had overtaken them?

The two types of quality

Quality, it is true, is a very important factor in competition. But quality has two definitions. One is conformance with specification. The other is fitness for purpose. They may look alike in some respects but my experience is that in practice they tend to pull in very different directions.

The first approach uses the standard as the guiding strategy. Where there are standards available on the performance of materials, for example as protection against flammability or corrosion, there is a firm starting base on which to tackle the design of a product. Otherwise, standards have to be invented. Here the Product Design Engineer has a far-reaching responsibility. The product or its components are commonly put out to tender and manufacturing tolerances need to be specified. In the absence of any specific guidelines or experience, the engineer will have to impose an arbitrary standard. Here it is safer to opt for caution so the tolerances are likely to be tight. That will set up a chain reaction of other engineers, managers and workers, possibly in a wide variety of establishments, struggling to conform to this now-stated standard of exactitude.

The second approach to quality follows a different strategy: it focuses on what is critical to function. That cannot be determined by a draughtsman. The starting point has to be nearer the customer; in fact, it can start with the customer, via market research. In the case of contractor–supplier relationships, it may entail visits to the firm that provided the contract (treating the documentation almost as a diversion). Here the user often turns out to be a different person, with different priorities, from the person who originally drew up the contract. The emphasis in the discussions will fall on areas where difficulty is being experienced. 'No, that tolerance is not really critical', said of a tolerance the supplier is finding it hard to fall within. And continuing: 'Our problem is with this dimension ... it affects the efficiency of our filling machines', about a fault the supplier can easily rectify.

One way of regarding quality is to assume that you can never know it all. Meeting the contract is not in the same league as outpacing the competition. Here the latter art is to be ahead of the game: it is to excel.

There is a difference between competence and excellence. One dictionary definition of competence is of a 'sufficiency that falls short of a superfluity'. There is a good enough standard to be expected in every job. Given enough good standards we have the perfectly competent employee. Just as standards and tolerances can specify quality, so also competencies can specify people for each and every job.

The path of excellence follows a different route. In the field of quality, it means seeking to establish what would constitute even better 'fitness for function'. Continuous probing, study and research will be needed for the answers. Once obtained, the answers may well conflict with 'the way we do things'. The neat procedures of Blue Work may become the principal forms of obstruction. There is a continuous struggle going on between those who are defending competence and those who are striving for excellence.

So why has excellence lost out in the struggle between values, and why is it that Blue Work has taken over? I can only speculate on the answer: it is that excellence has made a false start. Some years ago excellence had been thrust into prominence by Tom Peters's book *In Pursuit of Excellence* and more especially by Peters's evangelical advocacy in those mass meetings which the Spiritual Head of Management Education had conducted in many parts of the world. The message was that it was general value placed on excellence that accounted for the rise of firms to pre-eminence as world leaders. However, the message fell flat on its face as the fortunes of the cited companies nose-dived soon after the book was written.

The Spiritual Head now changed his tune by discovery of new managerial insights. And the attention of the world was duly diverted from the Great Message. However, the importance of Peters's original theme was too easily lost. What allows a firm to achieve ascendency and to maintain its position is a whole set of factors that can act in unison. But this pattern can change slowly, and sometimes almost imperceptibly, over time. Excellence can be overtaken and submerged by the prize of success and bigness with its offspring, bureaucracy. Tom Peters's intuition in pointing an index finger towards the pursuit of excellence should not be taken as being invalidated by the disappointments that followed.

Maintaining specified quality and finding new ways of excelling in quality involve contrasting strategies in the setting up of work. The former along with its attached 'competencies', now the output of a great new industry in management consultancy, falls firmly into the camp of Blue Work. But how should excellence be tackled?

The colour of excellence

There is only one thing certain about excellence: it is unlikely to be achieved by concentrating on Blue Work. Blue Work consolidates what has been achieved in the past. Blue Work may be the fruit of past excellence but that fruit now represents no more than standard performance. It may have mellowed but its special ripeness and sweet taste no longer marks it out as special.

The search for real excellence is likely to embrace people in three different forms of work – Yellow, Orange and White. They may work with a similar goal in mind in an abstract sense, especially if it is projected as quality, a term capable of being of conveying a common understanding among those in widely diverse occupations. But differences in the colour form in which the work is set up mean that it will be approached in characteristically different ways.

Where the objective is given a yellow hue, it has to be couched in a way that accepts that an advance falls within the bounds of individual accomplishment. A composer might be given a contract to write a new anthem for a state occasion or an architect might be invited to submit a design as part of a competition for a prestigious new building. Neither would receive such an invitation unless a personal reputation had already been established. Much the same position holds within industry. An engineer selected to investigate an unexplained loss of power from an industrial heating system will be chosen after due consideration has been given to how individually undertaken projects have been performed in the past. Competencies could provide a lead. But the selectors will be looking for something more – for signs of distinction.

The need for proven people in particular realms of accomplishment is less of a problem when a team is set up in order to prepare the way for a new advance, as, for example, in creating the design for an improved product. Greater latitude is permitted because, if the team is well balanced and its members compatible, the synergy of the team should be able to supply the energy and creativity needed. The work set up in this way will, of course, be Orange Work.

Advances in quality and in service or application may come about spontaneously if the culture is conducive to the pursuit of excellence. Quite specifically, this means that the work of employees needs to be set up in a way that permits, recognizes and encourages expansion.

That is why there must be room for White Work on the agenda of jobs. That is why the facilitator must work to extract that information from the jobholder and feed it back to the manager. In that way the White worker becomes eligible for later sanction as a Yellow Work assignment.

The risks of excellence

Excellence cannot be counted on as a commodity to be expected in the satisfactory employee. Excellence deserves no mention by its absence: it is notable only by its presence. The facilitator who assists in feeding back to the manager the interpretation of the briefing by the jobholder will ensure that the content of White and Yellow Work conveys the full quality of any contribution that has been made. In the case of Orange Work, the role of the facilitator is reduced. Any successful group should be able to handle successfully the outputs of their own deliberations unassisted. The way in which work is set up must allow scope for excellence and for excellence to show through once it is found.

Unfortunately there is a downside to excellence which occurs where it is associated with individual rather than group work. It is one of the findings of research into team roles that outstanding strengths often carry an associated weakness. In team work the weakness is termed allowable because other members are available to slot into complementary roles to cover the weakness. The result is that, as far as the outside world is concerned, the weakness may not show in practice. Where individual work is concerned, that compensatory mechanism may not be available. Striving for excellence may therefore put some aspects of the stability of the system at risk. For example, progress with the new sometimes leads to an unnecessarily aggressive attitude and an intolerance of the traditional. A White culture, comprising a research-based elite, in contending with a Blue culture will often act dismissively on the need for systematic measurement and the exercise of formal controls. A Blue culture, for its part, may defend a static conception of quality and remain oblivious to the adage that 'quality cannot be inspected into a product'. These battles may be fought out in personal terms. Different approaches to work generate their own values which can then take on a momentum of their own. The risks, however, ultimately depend on the players themselves. How the players respond to the variation of values encountered in an increasingly cosmopolitan work system will determine the pattern that shapes the overall culture.

If a movement from competence to excellence entails some risks, those risks will be judged worth taking as the pressures change. The deregulation and globalization of markets mean that competition will be forcing the pace. 'The best is only just good enough', may sometimes be said in mock humour. In due course it will be said in earnest.

In this chapter I have endeavoured to show that skills, competencies and the striving after excellence are construct models with a different history and associated with different approaches to the setting up of work. To some extent they will compete. And yet each has a place and a context in which to flourish.

Blue, White, Yellow and Orange Work have all been found relevant to the subject matter of this chapter. That is why the different work dispositions of jobholders need early recognition if management is to utilize effectively their separate contributions. The dynamic organization needs both stability and maintenance and the capacity to thrust forward with vigour, all at the same time.

13

Team roles and colour codes —

A team role is a characteristic way of behaving and contributing to a team and is very much dependent on the attributes of the person, whereas the assignment of work in terms of how that work should be carried out is subject to the authority and discretion of the manager. Managers have their own preferred styles. Some are domineering and autocratic, others believe in devolution and delegation or are keen to foster participation. They assign work therefore in different ways and also according to the different pressures and urgencies arising. It can therefore be largely a matter of chance as to whether the work that is distributed in a characteristic way along with an expectation as to how it should be carried out is appropriate to the favoured team roles of the person to whom the work is assigned. All is eventually revealed. The manager will observe that the worker is satisfactory or no good at the job.

It would be a big step forward if it could be known in advance whether a person was right for a particular work assignment or not. On my reckoning this would entail, to start with, an understanding of the theory of the breakdown of work (in this instance through its application in Workset) plus a knowledge of the team roles of the person. Finally there is the crucial question of the connection between the two. Here one is up against an issue of epistemology. How is the connection to be established between two language systems that are essentially different?

In the absence of specific research any connection between the two systems has to be a matter of conjecture. So the only option is to fall back on observation. Yet it cannot be observation in the casual sense, since functional roles (what the job demands) are easily confused with team roles (the sort of behaviour within the team to which an individual is disposed). Happily a better starting point exists. Through Interplace, with its comprehensive set of information and outputs on personal team-role patterns, we had a very large number of people stored within the system. So it was easy to find from individuals personally known to us, and with clear-cut team roles, an adequate sample who had exhibited a very positive disposition towards certain types of work coupled with a marked avoidance of other work. The demands of their jobs could also be revealed by the Job Requirement Exercise, a constituent of Interplace, and although this cruder approach differs from the analysis that Workset offers, a pretty good guess could be made as to its crucial components in colour terms.

While more study is needed if the relationship between team roles and the colours of Workset is to be given quantitative expression, our collected cases at least allowed us to reach some tentative conclusions.

Blue Work

Many blue-collar workers are engaged in Blue Work not out of choice but from economic pressures. In other words, it is the only work available to them. Often the work does not suit them and they declare 'Well, it is a living, isn't it?' On the other hand, there are those who love work of this type and gravitate towards it. These includes white-collar workers and various members of the salariat. The extent of their involvement is shown by their painstaking application, interest in and sense of commitment to what they are doing and their attachment to a form of work that others would find not appealing at all.

The naturals in Blue Work have team roles that fall into the category of Completer and/or Implementer. When both roles are combined in the same person, the effect is even more marked: they make such a success of Blue Work that they are welcomed by all and sundry, and deficiencies in other areas of working capacity tend to be overlooked. Specialists are also happy as a rule in Blue Work, but the proviso here is that it relates to their specialism. Within that context they show remarkable robustness and staying power. That is why, in cases of doubt, a reminder of its relevance to their profession or craft can work wonders.

Yellow Work

There are many people, especially executives, who will accept responsibility but decline to undertake prescribed tasks. Every task suggested to them will be converted in some way. They will find a way of contracting out of the task and incorporating it into some different approach, with a slightly different set of objectives: it will end in a position allowing more room for manoeuvre and decision making.

Those who show the greatest gravitation to Yellow Work are Shapers, Plants and Specialists. Again those who combine the above team roles, usually being any two of these three, will show the strongest inclination towards this work. There are others who like some Yellow Work but not too much of it. Coordinators fall especially into this group. A small amount of Yellow Work, for those who would otherwise be denied it, can always be sprinkled around by the manager to advantage. So it would be a mistake to imagine that blue-collar workers shun Yellow Work. Often they yearn for it, the more because it is denied them. An analysis of how blue-collar workers, now cast as jobholders, are interpreting their brief will be a surprise to many. Blue-collar workers may appear as a homogeneous body from afar but closer inspection will reveal a minority who like some measure of Yellow Work provided it is kept within bounds.

White Work

Any unusually high amount of White Work in a jobholder's work repertoire carries a double-edged message. One message spells out that the jobholder is not working on that which is sanctioned and requested; the second message is an announcement of creative energy. These work attributes, containing both positive and negative facets, tend to be interdependent. As with Yellow Workers, it is a cluster to be found mostly in Plants and Shapers and once again, where these team roles are combined, the effect is magnified. However, it needs to be borne in mind that Plants and Shapers engage in White Work for different reasons. For Plants the attraction lies in the appeal of doing something inventive and the satisfaction that comes from the result being 'all one's own work'. In the case of Shapers, White Work is very often a consequence of Pink Work. The Shaper does not wish to be idle and will find useful ways of filling unoccupied time and will not flinch from engaging in activities that are not part of the official agenda.

White Work is absent from the work profiles of many jobholders. Where it is to be found it usually occupies a very small amount of working time. Nevertheless, its size should not diminish its potential importance. The volume of White Work is a marker of local initiative; it provides a measure of the vigour going into continuous improvement.

Green Work

Most people ensure they have a certain amount of Green Work in the repertoire. Its attraction is that it offers a convenient means of satisfying social needs at work. There are, however, some people for whom it is more than a marginal activity. They prefer to work that way even when given a choice between a range of working activities. One common arrangement is for people to work in pairs. Moving a little further up the size range, some manufacturing activities allow for the rotation of workers between a number of different operations, so providing variety for themselves and versatility and adaptability for the firm.

However, the 'social module' system of task arrangement does not appeal to all. The main appeal of Green Work is to Resource Investigators (who get bored easily) and to Teamworkers (who like the reassurance and company of others). So its appeal can be for different reasons. Green Work has least appeal to Specialists. For them a combination of the indefinite nature of the activity and its usual low professional ranking can be a source of frustration.

Orange Work

Joint responsibility carries many advantages and few conspicuous disadvantages. People enjoy being in on a decision, especially if things go well; if things go wrong, there is less personal vulnerability. Only Specialists commonly dislike Orange Work unless their specialism becomes the focus of the meeting. Otherwise distaste for Orange Work stems from badly conducted meetings and from a failure of the person in charge to recognize the potential contribution and value of each member of the team. That is why people will get a lot out of some meetings while complaining about others. Orange Work is not worth setting up unless it can be managed with skill.

Orange Work, ideally, offers scope for all team roles provided the team has been composed on sound principles. Orange Work presents a great attraction to Coordinators. They are usually the team members who are capable of extracting value from this colour set.

Pink Work

I have established little evident affinity between Pink Work and any particular team roles. This is not to deny that some connection may be found in the future. For the moment it would seem that the volume of Pink Work is largely governed by the local culture and whatever happen to be the reactions of management once they learn that Pink Work exists and falls within their domain. Such situational factors cut across whatever team roles are to be found and therefore minimize their significance.

The only team role that, on limited evidence, does figure in Pink Work is that of Monitor Evaluator. Amid a general air of hustle and bustle it takes a clear and analytical mind to recognize that some activities are fruitless. The Monitor Evaluator is enough of a realist to differentiate between those activities that add value and those that do not. The Monitor Evaluator is the first to recognize Pink Work but also the first to assist in its elimination.

The reluctance of jobholders to identify Pink Work is understandable, for it could betoken a death warrant to the discoverer with its covert message 'I am not a very useful employee'. This is far from the case. The greater the amount of Pink Work revealed, the greater is the potential for improving labour productivity and effectiveness. In a sense, Pink Work is a signpost pointing to future wealth and prosperity even if the news in the short term looks bleak and discouraging.

Grey Work

I have not so far found any association between Grey Work and team roles. What a larger than average amount of Grey Work may imply is that the manager and the jobholder are somewhat out of touch with one another so that each perceives the job in somewhat different terms.

A general strategy for deploying team roles

The manager is in a position to consider, once an analysis of a job is completed, how knowledge of team roles might be used to make an inspired placement. If there were, in principle, a one-to-one relationship between the colour codes of the work analysed and the nine team roles, placement decisions would be easy. But matters are more complicated than that. In the first place, few jobs will be depicted by a single colour which would make the information relatively simple to act on. Second, individuals do not hold up a placard declaring their attachment to a particular team role nor do the records themselves. The Interplace data that many firms hold on the team roles of their employees will show a variation in affinity for each of the team roles. The focus of attention becomes the rank order in which these appear. That allows some answers to the question: how much affinity does a given employee have for each of the team roles? The team-role spectrum of an employee can therefore be related to the colour spectrum of the job given the arrival of the necessary technique for processing the material.

Until the techniques of matching are developed further, ambitions should be limited and the priority should more simply be one of avoiding a poor placement. For example, a Plant or Resource Investigator should not be assigned to a job where the colour is predominantly Blue: a Teamworker or a Completer should not be placed in a job which is predominantly Yellow: a Specialist should not be assigned to a job that is mainly Orange. In each case one would have to add 'Unless the secondary role fitted perfectly into what is required'.

The two spectra about people and work relate to one another at present in only a rudimentary way. But they relate well enough to enable obvious mistakes to be avoided.

Placements without team roles

Consider the case where there is no knowledge of team roles. Yet a transfer placement needs to be made. Here the starting point is to build up for an employee a history of performance in the job or even in several jobs, if that employee has moved around within the firm. A comparison between how the job was set up and how it is being performed will offer leads on how much the individual employee is contributing to the colour shift. This has important implications. For example, an employee who increases the amount of Green Work in a job should be moved towards a job where Green Work is the main feature. It is not incumbent to become involved in the language of team roles. But suppose the point at issue is less the demands of a particular job as such but considerations of a working partnership. Suppose the appointee will need to work with a talented Shaper Specialist whose work is taking on a partly social character. And let us consider that the primary character is a difficult person with whom to work.

What sort of team role would this position require? Perhaps a Teamworker/Coordinator. By using the Interplace system such a person could be identified from the database within seconds. But let us assume the firm does not possess Interplace and no such data are available. The only information relates to Workset. Here the person being considered has a record of shifting assigned work in the direction of the Green and the Orange. That pattern shift is as strongly indicative of a needed Teamworker/Coordinator as one might wish and here there is every prospect of making an excellent placement.

Given a certain amount of experience and training, the colour code of the jobholder can be handled in such a way that it interfaces with team-role theory and language. The two systems are moving towards a single unitary system. That movement will not be completed without further research and must in any case await the intended computerization of Workset.

14

Managers and leaders revisited ──────────

A manager was defined in Chapter 1 as a person who assigns tasks and responsibilities to others. That definition is as eloquent about what it leaves out as about what it says. There is no mention of those supposedly quintessential managerial activities – communicating, motivating, organizing and setting objectives.

Such omissions are intentional, while at the same time I readily concede that the casting of the role of a manager in a broader framework has served a valuable purpose, especially in an educational sense. The explanation of the omission in my definition is that the manager's role has changed somewhat in recent years. Many of those activities that fell into the everyday domain of the manager have now become shared with an assortment of well-educated executives. These comprise technical experts and advisers and a rainbow of professionals, including human resource professionals and those who carry the title of Management Development without being in a managerial position themselves. Managers are urged to be masters of communication. But communication has become a professional business too. Managers employ specialists, including and especially outside contractors, to communicate to the public and often to their customers. Similarly managers bring in professionals to communicate even to their own workers: former journalists are engaged in editing company newsletters. Consulting firms are given assignments to probe the attitudes of the staff towards the company. And industrial relations officers play their part in handling issues arising at the workplace at the oral level, while also advising managers on those extrinsic reward systems that will keep the workforce well motivated and working. Organizing can be made the core activity of scheduling clerks. Where direction of effort is concerned, managers are finding responsibility for setting objectives taken over by directors, many of whom have no managerial duties, most notably in the case of part-time members of a board. Such restrictions affecting the general scope of managers are greater still in the case of public bodies where objectives are often set by external regulating bodies or by government itself.

While the relative numbers of these varied executives have increased, they are not necessarily in command of anyone in the sense that they have subordinates to whom tasks and responsibilities can be assigned. Managers, in the sense in which I have defined them, have become a dwindling minority which has had cultural consequences. The flattening of hierarchy in opening up opportunities to non-managerial executives has helped to create resistance to the authority and status of the manager–boss. Hence it is scarcely surprising that some of the leading management thinkers of our day have taken the current position one step further and have jibbed at the continued use of the word manager. Instead they have transferred their approval to the blander terms, associate and executive, and have encouraged their wider use.

What is the colour of a manager's job?

Nevertheless, I have clung steadfastly to the concept of the manager, even in its more restricted sense, because I think we cannot live without it. The workers expect it. They will refer to management, even where it is conspicuous by its absence or treated with scepticism where visible. They look for leadership, even if they dislike being led. Managers and leaders may be the subject of a love–hate relationship on the part of workers but they have an omnipresence in the workplace. The emotional ambivalence associated with these titles will continue until a change in the meaning of the words intrudes into the unconscious and eventually occupies a settled place in the public mind. That has happened before. A precedent has been set in the case of the word 'king'. That once all-powerful autocrat has become the benign monarch who can wield no more than symbolic power. Human language is dynamic. Words can eventually acquire a meaning not far short of the opposite of their origin. In this situation of continuing flux, what we need to re-establish is the meaning of the manager. Once re-established, that meaning needs to be consolidated.

It is here that Workset may help in clarifying meaning, just as it has done so in the case of jobholders. Are managers jobholders and, if so, can the job of the manager be usefully defined by the same colour code? Does the arrangement of particular hues allow us to proceed beyond the abstract and tell us something about how the manager's job is being performed?

Here the contraction of the manager's job makes the subject easier to appreciate now that it has been shorn of many of the associated activities. What is left to managers, and exclusively to managers, may have diminished. But the assigning of tasks, responsibilities and contracts (in the case of the larger organization) constitutes a cluster of duties of enormous magnitude that cannot be taken away. The manager's work now being made less diffuse is more open to an intimate analysis.

The job of the manager has not in fact lost its key position although the interpretation of that job by the manager, as a jobholder, may vary. In general terms, the colour of the job may be represented as being broadly yellow and orange, though it will contain occasional patches of blue and green. The aim of the efficient manager is to reduce the amount of blue and green which arrives in the in-tray in ever-increasing quantities. Some of this load can be lessened by assigning Blue Work to ancillary staff. But by assigning Yellow Work to invited and selected people, that is by delegating responsibility, the manager will greatly increase the offloading of onerous duties and thereby will gain more space and time in which to concentrate on core work.

Given the possibilities that now exist for greater freedom in their interpretation of the job, whether these are exercised or not, managers have three ways of addressing the challenges that face them.

One is to plunge for all-Yellow Work. Decoded, the message reads 'I am the decider. Bring me the information on all matters of importance and I will make the decisions.' Given such a demand, there will be a queue of people outside the manager's office waiting to come in.

The second approach is to mix Yellow and Green Work. In effect, this hands-on style means that the manager is readily drawn towards every important happening where decisions can be made on the spot. This style is commonly termed 'firefighting'. Fittingly, one can imagine the manager with a large fire hose directing its contents with unfailing energy at whatever is seen as a problem.

The third, and perhaps the most productive of the styles, has a larger social content; it comprises combining the yellow and the orange modes of working. In other words, the manager will have some work expressed as a personal responsibility but will also share responsibility with others. Exactly how the two combine often becomes a critical matter. The obstacle, where others are concerned, is plain enough: it will not be clear where Orange and Yellow Work start and end, unless particular people have worked with a particular manager for a very long time. An even more serious situation occurs when the manager has failed to think through the distinction in terms of a desirable self-management strategy.

Take the case of a sales manager who departs on an overseas trip to an unknown but potentially important customer. The sales manager makes unexpected progress in the negotiation and returns with a big order. So far, so good. However, closer examination of the contract reveals that the keen price agreed for the volume of the order raises issues about whether the assumed economies of scale can be profitably achieved. A second problem is whether the productive capacity exists to fulfil the order in time to meet the deadline for delivery. A triumph can soon turn into a disaster. If the latter, there will be an inquest and the sales manager will be charged with exceeding his or her authority. To that there is an obvious reply 'I was expected to win major contracts and to expand the business and that is exactly what I have achieved.'

I have encountered that and similar situations on many occasions. The reason why the problem arises is that the two types of responsibility, yellow and orange, are not distinguished in the way in which work is set up. Job specifications have become largely definitions of personal territory. To share or not to share: that is the problem. And here job specifications offer few clues.

The change towards the increasingly interdependent nature of work means that an interface will always need to be found between personal work and the work of those in adjacent areas. Here there are advantages in positioning the manager's job in much the same way as that of any other senior professional. Like an accountant or an engineer, the manager is there to make a very distinctive contribution. Its importance is underlined, first, by the fact that the manager is the person to set up the terms of reference for and to select a team. Second, through self-assignment the manager may choose whether to join, or not to join, the team. Once in the team there should be some diminution in the manager's authority. The manager's decisions will no longer carry the same weight unless the team is dealing specifically with the assigning of tasks and responsibilities. Otherwise, rank should no longer count in the same way as outside the team. If it does, it becomes a potential impediment to performance and the team can soon slip into becoming a led group. Ideally, the manager is, or should be, simply another team member while retaining accountability for the performance of the team. What this means in practice is that the manager must adapt to a duality of roles. One is the functional role. That role is, by definition, to 'assign tasks and responsibilities to others'. The second role is the team role. The team role is the way in which a person behaves and contributes to a team both as a result of personal disposition and from a perception of the role of other team players. I have written about the nature of these roles elsewhere (*Team Roles at Work*, Butterworth-Heinemann, 1993) and the intention here is not to discuss them but to point out that a manager may be disposed towards or be reluctant to engage in any one of these roles. That inclination depends on being a particular person not on being a manager.

The conclusion is that in the new era into which we are moving a manager has a job which is gaining in clarity. But that job is not as a boss. Beyond the specifics of the job which by its nature is of more than average importance, the manager will be part of a network of executives: all will be interacting with one another.

Is there a role for a leader?

While the numbers of jobs available to managers have diminished due to delayering, there appears, in contrast, to have been increased interest in courses for would-be leaders. Strategic leadership, creative leadership and team leadership have all gained ground as subjects for the aspiring. The consequence could be a proliferation of people who see themselves as leaders and try to behave in the manner that the title leads others to expect. Quite what effect this would have within a single organization is best left to the imagination.

Any serious thoughts about the nature of leadership must first try to establish what the term means under contemporary conditions. Problems stem from the fact that the word leader can be used in one of two ways. A leader can refer to a person of rank who must be followed and who ideally has the necessary aptitude or, if not, can be trained to behave in a way expected for that position. However, a shift in meaning away from rank now takes us in almost the opposite direction. As the authority of management has allegedly been whittled away and as executives have become more equal, some claim the need for leadership has increased so that direction is not lost. Arguably there is a need for someone from within a group of broadly equal people who can stand up and stand out to fill the void and provide the necessary lead.

Here there is a clear implication that leadership is not part of the job but a quality that can be brought to a job. If so, how could one describe its colour?

The work that leadership encompasses in this context clearly is not assigned but comes about spontaneously. The core colours of blue, yellow, green and orange must therefore be ruled out along with their Grey borders. What is left is white and pink. And here the residual colour scheme fits perfectly.

The leaders who emerge, often from humble or obscure origins, are individuals who have created their own agenda and have then succeeded in transferring it to the masses. What their vision or dreams have created, whether for better or for worse, is White Work. Pink Work too is notable in creating the space from which the White can emerge. Many of those who achieved fame as political leaders have served long periods in prison, great religious prophets have sprung to the fore after solitary wanderings in the desert, many classic artists and musicians have spent long periods living in sordid conditions, unrecognized and without employment. The idleness of incarceration and isolation and seemingly unoccupied time provide the settings for nurturing a new vision. The pink gives rise to the white.

Relationships between leaders and managers

The restricted meaning of the word leader to refer to someone who creates and succeeds in passing on a new agenda would help to clear away the confusion that the term usually creates. However, that is not the way in which the word is customarily used. Leader more usually refers to someone who through force of personality is inclined to dominate others. That concept has given rise in the famed and wistful report of a manager about a staff member: 'He is not a born leader yet.' The charismatic leader is seen as the person to follow.

The term team leader is an oxymoron. It is a matter of concern that organizations that are continuously seeking team leaders are, often unknowingly, perpetuating the concept of the leader of a type incompatible with good teamwork. In effect, it is another way of referring to the boss of a group.

The charismatic leader, especially one self-proclaimed, has the effect of undermining the readiness of team members to think for themselves and to take an independent line. When it comes to efficiency the precedents are not encouraging. Many famed leaders have failed to reach the point of being even average in their managerial ability, in the sense of my definition, so that the more talented members of their entourage often act as though in despair. The quality of being a supposedly superior being, standing above immediate conventions and pressures, creates a certain social distance that works against close and sensitive interpersonal relationships. Yet leaders are customarily cast in a role in which they are expected to manage and to manage well, an illusion fostered by the awe in which they are generally held.

Managers who are skilled in assigning tasks and responsibilities would be better placed to manage leaders than leaders are to manage managers. But as the former are superior in rank, there would be a difficulty in opting for such an inversion.

Those considered by their team as true team leaders are barely distinguishable in practice from good team managers. Any distinction is basically a matter of context. Here the point can be illustrated in relation to the teachings of John Adair, the first appointee to a Chair in Leadership in the United Kingdom. One of his most widely used and admired models of leadership relates to his concept of three 'sets' in a leader's work. One is a focus on the needs of the individual, the second on the needs of the group and the third on the needs of the task. Keeping the three in balance is an important personal attribute which can be taught and developed. Outdoor courses provide a suitable setting and here leadership training is the acknowledged title for this approach. Once the lessons are transferred from a remote spot to the workplace, the subject and the skills are assimilated into management.

On such a reckoning there is no fundamental distinction between leadership and management ability and the redundancy in terminology could be a source of confusion. Should, however, the term leader be retained in its most distinctive meaning, as considered earlier, to apply to the charismatic visionary type, the problem becomes one of how leaders and managers should relate to one another.

There is always the possibility that the charismatic leader and the most able manager will succeed in forming a partnership and find an ideal way of combining their respective roles. An element of humility is required in both if such a partnership is to hold. The likelihood that this will happen is not high.

There is, however, a final solution for attempting to combine the irreconcilable. That is, one or the other will have to go. Earlier I have looked at the much-favoured case for dropping the term manager but have stated the reason why I think its retention is desirable. The other possibility is to drop the concept of the leader, an alternative that on balance seems decidedly preferable. That would encourage the manager to search for a more collectively-based solution to fill the void. If a replacement of that function can be found, a great step forward would be taken in lowering the risks attached to the worship of a single person. Whether that is feasible or not depends on the state of education of the public. If people look for and want to worship a great leader, one will certainly appear upon the scene, however misplaced that confidence may ultimately turn out to be.

A strategy for managers

If the central focus of a manager's job is to assign tasks and responsibilities to others, it is axiomatic that changing the way we work will be accomplished not by ourselves, as mere employees, so much as by management's discretion in the exercise of their prime responsibilities. The manager's commission is to draw up the contract, whether written or communicated orally. The contract may allow the employee only limited latitude or it may be expressed in a way that offers scope for expansion. The consequences will be considerable. Every appointment, every redrawing of job frontiers, every transfer of a person from one function to another has the potential to generate ripple effects that can extend to the far corners of an organization. The paradox for the manager is how to fulfil the personal responsibility for assigning work with the need both to consult colleagues and to win commitment for the validity of whatever processes are put into place.

For this social feature of a manager's job to be successfully encompassed the manager must create Orange Work, whether or not such work involves the self as a participant. The benefits of this recommendation may be illustrated by one personal experience on an occasion when I was invited to talk to a large hospital group. The chief executive was an unexpectedly young woman whose promotion had come from within and whose background had been administration. Though morale in the National Health Service at the time was notoriously low, in this hospital I could scarcely fail to sense the comradeship and general enthusiasm. The chief executive explained the strategy she had come to adopt in her rising career and confessed: 'I spend most of my time setting up well-balanced teams. I then just leave them to get on with it.'

The manager is not only setting up the contract for others but setting up the contract for the self. Here the manager is uniquely placed. No other employed professional or executive is in a position to withdraw personally from tasks and responsibilities by passing them on to others, for any act of work distribution or delegation is in itself managerial, whether a person regards the self as managerial or not. Assigning the right tasks and the right responsibilities to the right people is the essence of what the job of a manager is all about. But it is a burden that should not be borne alone. A formula must be found whereby the execution of that responsibility draws on consultation procedures that are clear to all. Meeting the demands of the job necessitates skill in handling an intricate and sometimes elusive network in which communication and interpersonal understanding will always play a critical part.

15

A way forward ─────────────────────

As I have become older I have had to run faster (figuratively speaking) in order to maintain an output commensurate with a realistic assessment of the working life that remains before me. The research which culminated in the development of team-role theory and which saw the light of day in *Management Teams: Why They Succeed or Fail* took nine years to complete; its successor *Team Roles At Work*, dealing with industrial applications, was published ten years later; while the use of Interplace as a computer-based expert system became well established in the international field some years further on. In other words, the process linking research and delivery was lengthy, extending over a period of a quarter of a century. Such a time span can hardly be afforded under current circumstances. In contrast, the material brought together in this book, linking the generation of an idea, research and development, pilot trials and the initial installation in large establishments of a radically new system of setting up and developing jobs has taken no more than three and a half years.

This quickening of pace owes much to the fact that the earlier studies and the widespread use to which they had been put had removed much of the unwillingness of prospective users to experiment with related new ventures. One key message had gained increased acceptance. That message was that long-term factors governing success in many jobs have less to do with specific knowledge and competencies and are more about role behaviour, orientation, aptitude and interest. Given confidence in the importance of these latter factors, appropriate training and experience could be provided to offer as candidates for jobs those considered to have undiscovered potential. As managers appreciated the merit of what we termed suitability (personal fitness for the job), as distinct from eligibility (qualifications and directly related experience), it became a short step to obtain their cooperation in a revised strategy for human resource management. A new starting point was made with jobs: that meant setting them up in a way that could take account of and respond to the individual characteristics of job occupants and job applicants.

The problem now was to put ideas to the test. Each year we held a conference in Cambridge for Interplace users, which drew participants from many parts of the world, and from that facility we found volunteers from a cross-section of national cultures to try out pilot programmes. So no serious time gap intervened between envisaging possibilities of advance and availing ourselves of the opportunity and prospects. In fact, the number of offers to provide facilities for pilot trials soon encouraged us to enter the next stage, comprising sponsored pilots. Since these pilot trials needed to finance themselves, a higher level of commitment was needed on the part of management. That commitment, once secured, had the effect of hastening the practical application of the ideas underlying the venture.

It was gratifying to find such positive attitude in the industrial firms, with which we had an association, towards the new approach. Yet we did not want to lose sight of the fact that the concepts underlying Workset originated as a response to the problems experienced in the National Health Service. Here the condition under which the service operates means that approved technique and practice enjoy a semi-independent existence alongside notions of ultimate medical responsibility.

The question of authority always poses problems. Historically, hospitals owe their organizational origins to the army in the field to which they were once accountable, for mass casualties needed to be treated systematically and they were handled in the expected military manner. The commanding officers of the medical world were men, assisted by nurses (women) who carried out the tasks prescribed for them. The gender stereotype, along with the associated command structure, remained in place for a long time. But increasingly that general position was coming under strain. The forces making for change were that women were moving into jobs of increased professional standing and that advances in both medicine and treatment called for increased interdisciplinary teamwork which cut across notions of hierarchy. The resulting disarray and susceptibility to misunderstandings undermined morale. Yet no solutions emerged.

Several groups of representatives from the National Health Service attended the seminars I conducted, and yet the immediate prospects of conducting pilot experiments in the public service were not good. The basic reason is that the public service is always subject to political complications and no step forward is possible without an appreciable amount of slow-moving negotiation and, commonly, entrenched opposition from one quarter or another.

It was therefore a matter of considerable pleasure for us that, as if in compensation for the absence of hospitals in our pilot studies, one hospital became an active supporter of our sponsored pilot pro-gramme and provided excellent facilities. That did not mean that everything we desired could be taken for granted. Senior clinical staff cannot be dragooned into taking part in new developments that are essentially managerial in nature and, for that very reason, they are more likely to be resisted by those who see themselves first and foremost as professionals. The readiness to volunteer is a prerequisite to getting started. Here again we were blessed by the participation of a medical department that had already gained general recognition for its professional standing and general efficiency.

Due to our belief that we could not train facilitators until we had learned to become facilitators ourselves, my partner, Barrie Watson, and I set about dividing the work in this hospital between us. My very first case revolved round the work of a team leader in an operating theatre. The manager, to whom the team leader was accountable, provided a synopsis of the duties and expressed a view on how tasks and responsibilites were best separated. I then strove to assign the various functions into the four colour sets and in consultation with the manager formulated the words that could best encapsulate their essential nature. Eventually I arrived at a comprehensive write-up that comprised just 175 words.

Just as we were about to close our meeting, the manager said 'I don't know whether you would care to see the job specification which we already have for this particular job'. Naturally I assented. Whereupon he produced a substantial document which I promised I would take away to read at leisure. It so happened that at the weekend we were holding a garden party for family and friends. Barrie was himself attending in order to allow us an occasion in which to discuss the hospital results. As part of the analysis of the job I set about counting the number of words used in the job specification. The pages ran to eleven and the number of words was approximately 2750, although I would not like to guarantee the actual number to the nearest five to ten since to count every word on every page stressed my attention capacity. If the document was arduous to count, I suspect it was equally arduous to read. My daughter, who was visiting us with her family and who had once been a ward sister in a leading London hospital, asked if she could also see the documentation. When the perusal was over, she exclaimed 'It's a funny thing, but after reading all that material, I still don't have a clear picture of the job'.

Here I had occasion to reflect. Do more words create more understanding? Or is the contrary the case? Too many words may reduce understanding. A reminder here is our drawer full of technical manuals relating to all the equipment we have ever had for our domestic appliances and for our office. In retrospect I realized that the larger the manual, the less ready we have been to consult it. With the larger manuals it usually takes an inordinate time to find the information you seek. Expressed as what is known in psychology as information theory, it is all a matter of signal/noise ratio. The information one seeks is the signal: all the rest is the noise. The most efficient communication depends on maximizing the signal and minimizing the noise. In the case of equipment there is always the temptation to resort to trial and error in order to test its functioning if by so doing one can avoid the need to read unnecessarily long instructions. The oversize manual then lies doomed to remain unread within its promising but disappointing covers.

While the discussion on the hospital job was proceeding the nature of the extensive specification aroused the curiosity of a friend of mine who wandered up to our table. His reaction was one of instant recognition. A former architect in the Cambridge City Corporation, he immediately named the likely management consultants and declared eighteen years ago it had been proposed that his job should be 'done' in a similar way. 'The whole of local government went over to this particular system,' he declared. 'Yes, I know the next step in using this information: all these competencies get transformed into points which then by some involved process place the job in a particular pay grade. "It's rubbish", my friend, an outspoken Yorkshireman, reportedly told his boss. "No", said the then chief executive of the corporation. "It's the pattern of the future".' My friend thereupon decided to quit the service of the corporation and set up his own, ultimately very successful, architectural practice.

There are not many people in local government who are quite as forthright as my friend. Nor, for that matter, are management consultants themselves as frank as they might be. My public critique of current practices, whether in a private or public context, has not been rebutted by management consultants I have met, nor by those who run training and educational courses for aspiring managers, nor by executives in large corporations whether in the private or public sector. They have often been embarrassed by what is said but refrained from rising to the intellectual challenge. Sometimes they show themselves very ready to agree but add, almost apologetically 'There is a lot of business in this field'; or 'our courses on this subject are well attended'.

The undoubted reality is that there are many executives and professionals in the human resource field whose standing and career prospects depend on their grip over an elaborate bureaucratic process, that in the wider context offers little of value. Dismantling this system might be considered a desirable step. And yet such an intention is not easy to put into operation. Any excision of one part of the system will have implications for the rest. Whenever the complex payment arrangements of a large organization depends on a particular source of information, that information is afforded a certain sanctity. Any disturbance to that source material can be seen as threatening the financial security of the denizens of the organization itself and so bring into being a mounting backlash.

That was the trap into which we unwittingly fell in our initial pilot studies. We had been welcomed with open arms into one large company that was seemingly keen to strike out on the path of change and progress. For a while our work went as we would have wished. Then by chance we stumbled upon the most complex system of job evaluation we had ever seen. But for all that, it was still the system that governed everybody's earnings. What we had witnessed and what we were introducing were clearly incompatible and it was surely only a matter of time before the issue came to a head. And when it did, the struggle took place behind closed doors. We were never privy to what took place. All we knew was that those who had sponsored our introduction fell from grace. We felt sorry that their willingness to investigate better ways of doing things had led them into conflict with the status quo and we resolved to be more careful in choosing future partners for our trials.

The lesson is that a system needs to be viewed as a whole before any decision is made to alter one of its parts. Evolution by stealth is not a workable option. A paradigm shift is a big step for any company. There is little prospect that such a shift can be successfully undertaken until all the possible advantages and disadvantages are discussed not only with senior management but with those likely to be affected one way or another. Nothing can be presumed. No venture relating to the organization of jobs starts with a blank sheet. There will always be custom and practice, a formal means or an informal one, whereby jobs are brought into being.

This is a field that has been very little studied. Companies are often unaware how jobs are set up: in their view it happens in some mysterious way which is difficult to describe. In other cases, managers confidently report on a process that bears only a superficial resemblance to what happens in practice so that it is common to find little correspondence between the perception of managers, especially those in senior positions, and the perception of employees. Clearly questions need to be asked. Appendix 2 offers a method of auditing existing practices in job setting and aims at generating comparative information. The stimulus to reform is an awareness of shortcomings, and, if there are serious deficiencies, they will surely be exposed by proper investigation. Only then will the need for intervention be likely to be seen.

The stark fact is that segmented jobs, the cellular structures and the demarcation that exists within large organizations have been created by design. Managers must bear much of the blame, for they have connived in the generation of routine procedures and a large amount of unusable paperwork which lies at the heart of slow-moving and wasteful bureaucracies. Since there will be many executives who have an entrenched interest in what is already there, I do not foresee any prospect of sudden change. But I am sure the experiments we have undertaken will continue at a mounting pace and in different settings. And from those outcomes an eventual paradigm shift may usher in an era offering greater fulfilment for working communities.

Appendix 1

A glossary of terms ─────────

Blue Work Tasks that need to be carried out in a prescribed way to an approved standard.
Core Work Assigned work, whether Blue, Yellow, Green or Orange.
Executive An employee with a broad span of responsibility.
Facilitator One who guides the manager and jobholder through the Workset process.
Green Work Assigned tasks varying in their execution according to local circumstances and relationships.
Grey Work Unassigned work related to Core Work but deviating from it. Often arises as a response to contingencies.
Job Casting The manager's view of the job as conveyed to the Jobholder.
Jobholder An employee who is given a blend of tasks and responsibilities.
Leader One who gives direction and causes others to follow (may apply to the 'natural' leader but also may include the demagogue and the dictator).
Manager One who assigns tasks, responsibilities and contracts to others.
Orange Work Shared responsibility. Also covers instances where members of a team decide how the work should be distributed among themselves.
Pink Work Work which demands the presence of the jobholder but yields no useful results. Time is considered by the jobholder to be largely wasted.
Team member One with a distinctive role to play while sharing with designated others a common purpose.
White Work Unassigned work initiated by the jobholder.
Worker An employee who is given tasks.
Work Loss The general tendency for the jobholder to spend less time than expected on certain types of work. Work Loss comprises:

Significant omissions – Failure to carry out important aspects of the job due to other pressures. *Neglected work* – Omissions attributable to personal disinterest or disinclination on the part of jobholder. *Obsolete work* – Assigned work for which there is no longer a continuing need.

Workset An interactive system, using colour, designed to develop jobs and to improve communications between managers and jobholders.

Work Shift The general tendency for the jobholder to spend more time than expected on certain types of work. Work Shift comprises: *Excessive focus* – More time is spent on part of the job than would seem justified. *Demand drift* – The nature of the work reflects changing client or customer demands. *Discovered work* – Useful work that the Jobholder has personally created.

Yellow Work An assigned responsibility for which an individual is held accountable. Exactly how the work is tackled does not matter too much as long as the goal is achieved.

Appendix 2

Workset – audit of existing practices in job setting ─────────

This questionnaire has been designed to identify current methods and practices in setting up jobs. **It is for completion by jobholders.**

Question 1   Date: _____

Question 2   Name of organization: _____

Question 3   Department: _____

Question 4   How long have you been in your current job? (Please tick one box only)

    1   ☐   Less than 3 months
    2   ☐   3 to 12 months
    3   ☐   1 to 2 years
    4   ☐   Longer than 2 years

Question 5   Which of the following most accurately describes your situation? (Please tick one box only)

    1   ☐   My job existed prior to my appointment
    2   ☐   My job existed but was modified at the time of my appointment
    3   ☐   I was appointed to a new job that didn't previously exist

Question 6 Which of the following were used to explain the nature of your job? (Please tick the appropriate box or boxes)

1 ☐ A written Job Description (giving a general explanation of the job)
2 ☐ A written Job Specification (itemizing the duties covered and competences required)
3 ☐ Detailed oral instructions
4 ☐ Brief oral outline and physical on-the-job demonstration
5 ☐ Other (please describe)

Question 7 Which of the following would be your preferred method of having your job explained to you? (Please tick the appropriate box or boxes)

1 ☐ A written Job Description (giving a general explanation of the job)
2 ☐ A written Job Specification (itemizing the duties covered and competences required)
3 ☐ Detailed oral instructions
4 ☐ Brief oral outline and physical on-the-job demonstration
5 ☐ Other (please describe)

Question 8 How frequently is your job normally reviewed? (Please tick one box only)

1 ☐ Never
2 ☐ Seldom
3 ☐ Occasionally
4 ☐ At frequent intervals

Question 9 When modification to your job takes place which of the following procedures normally apply? (Please tick the appropriate box or boxes)

1 ☐ New documentation is provided for you
2 ☐ The modifications are explained to you orally
3 ☐ You exercise discretion in modifying the job without resorting to formal procedures
4 ☐ Other (please describe)

Question 10 How satisfied are you with existing practices for setting up and developing jobs? (Please tick one box only)

1 ☐ Very satisfied
2 ☐ Fairly satisfied
3 ☐ Unsure
4 ☐ None too satisfied
5 ☐ Very dissatisfied

Question 11   If you ticked boxes 4 or 5 when answering question 10 please briefly explain below why you are less than satisfied.

_____

_____

_____

_____

_____

Question 12   Which of the following statements most accurately describes how you feel about your job? (Please tick one box only)

1   ☐   It gives me a high level of personal satisfaction
2   ☐   It gives me a fair amount of personal satisfaction
3   ☐   It would need modifying quite a bit to make it appealing to me
4   ☐   It is a lot less appealing than other jobs within the organization I feel I am capable of doing
5   ☐   I do not like the job, although I do it to the best of my ability

Question 13   How easy is it for you to have discussions with your manager about your job? (Please tick one box only)

1   ☐   Very easy
2   ☐   Fairly easy
3   ☐   None too easy
4   ☐   Very difficult

Index ─────────────────────────────

Accountability:
    horizontal, 77–80
    vertical, 77, 80
Authority, 103
Avoidance reaction, 24

Belbin, Meredith, 9, 10
Blue Work:
    composition, 32
    definition, xi, 17
    past excellence standard, 85
    setting standards, 82–3
    team roles, 89
    underscoring, 64–5
    work element wording, 44
Bridges, William, 25, 32

Carver, Barney, 9
Colour coding:
    mix analysis, 61–2
    principles, xi–xii, 23
    role in culture language, 75
Colour sets, 17, 23
Commands, 2
Competence, 84–5
Completers, 89
Conferring, 52
Connolly, Jim, 9
Contractor–supplier relationships, 83
Coordinators, 90, 91, 93
Cranfield Management School, 9
Culture, see Industrial culture

Departmentalism, 13
Discovered work, 46
Discovery Method, see Guided Discovery
    Method of Training
Disorder, causes, 2–4
Drucker, Peter, 25

Educating, 52
Ergonomics, 10–11
Excellence:
    aims, 84–5
    consequences, 86

Facilitator, 104
    quantifying role, 57–8
    role, 37–9, 41, 55–6
    Workset role, 48–9
Facilitator's Manual, 38
Feedback, 33
    management, 63–4
    quantification, 57–8, 62
    requirements, 53–4
Freedom, employees', 32

Gilbreth, Lillian, 10
Gradualism, see Guided Discovery
    Method of Training
Green Work:
    composition, 32–3
    definition, xi, 18
    manager's role, 96

team roles, 90–1
time allocation, 61
underscoring, 65
work element wording, 44
Grey Work:
  definition, xi, 21, 51
  feedback use, 45, 46–7, 53–4
  scope, 54–5, 66–7
  team roles, 92
Guided Discovery Method of Training,
  36–7

Hammer, Michael, 25–6
Harper, Lance, 9
Hills, Seymour, 10
Human engineering, 10–11
Human Resource Management System
  (Interplace), 72, 103

Implementers, 89
In Attendance Workset, 22–3, 46
Industrial culture, 69–71
  adapting, 73–4
  developing, 71–2
  organizational, 30–1
  use of colour coding, 74–5
Innovation:
  barriers, 34–5
  communications strategy, 36–7
Instructing, 52
Instructions, 2, 46
Interplace, *see* Human Resource
  Management System
Interpretation response, 24

Job briefing:
  preparation, 41–5, 64
  presentation, 45–7
Job casting, 40
Job description, 12, 13
Job evaluation, 12–13
Job specification, 12, 13, 96, 104–5
Job titles, 13
Jobholder:
  colour allocation, 43–4
  estimator's role, 38–9
  responses by, 54–5
  time expenditure measurement, 60–1
  Workset role, 48–9
Jobholder assessment sheet, 53–4
Jobholder return sheet, 55

Jobs:
  concept, 8, 25–7
  division, 27–9
  scope, 29–30

Language:
  meaning, 16
  usage, 70–1
Leadership, 98–9, *see also* Team leaders

Management by exception, 58
Management model, 3–4, 5
Manager:
  job colour, 95–8
  job explanation, 31–2
  job strategy, 100–1
  leadership skills, 99–100
  role, 1, 25–6, 41, 94–5
  Workset role, 48–9
Monitor Evaluator, 91–2
Motivation, 26

Negotiating, 52
Non-core activities, 20–3

Orange Work:
  composition, 32
  definition, xi, 18–20
  excellence objective, 85
  manager's role, 96
  team empowerment, 76
  team roles, 91
  underscoring, 65
  work element wording, 44–5
Orders, 1–2

Payment systems, 35
Peripheral work, 46
Person images, 5–7
Peter, Tom, 84
Pink Work:
  definition, xii, 23
  feedback use, 45, 46–7, 53–4
  scope, 54, 66–7
  team roles, 91–2
Plants, 89, 90

Quality:
  definitions, 83
  standards, 82

Re-engineering, 13, 25–6
Resource Investigators, 91
Responsibilities:
  composition, 16
  devolution, 80

Scientific Management, 8, 12
Selling, 52
Semler, Ricardo, 26
Senge, Peter, 25
Shapers, 89, 90
Shaw, Ann, 10
Skills Analysis, 81
  and standards, 82–3
Specialists, 89
Standards, 82–3
Structure, employees, 32

Task:
  composition, 16
  images, 6–7
Taylorism, *see* Scientific Management
Team empowerment, 76–7
  training for, 79
Team leaders, 99–100
Teamwork, 13
  deployment strategy, 92–3
  roles, 88–9, 102
  transfer placements, 93
Teamworkers, 91, 93
Therbligs, 10, 11
Time expenditure measurement, 58–60, 64
Time keys, 59
Time study, 11

Unplanned work classification, 66–8

White Work:
  composition, 32
  definition, xi, 21–2
  excellence objective, 85
  feedback use, 45, 46–7, 68
  scope, 54, 67–8, 86
  team roles, 90
Work:
  allocation, 26
  classification, 14, 16
  measurement, 11
  organization, 27–9
Work study, *see* Human engineering
Workset:
  approved verbs, 51–2
  audit questionnaire, 110–12
  basis, 20
  choice of colours, xi
  commercial version, 113
  information flow, 48–9

Yellow Work:
  composition, 32
  definition, xi, 17
  excellence objective, 85
  manager's role, 96
  team roles, 89–90
  time allocation, 60–1
  underscoring, 65
  work element wording, 44–5

AUTHOR'S NOTE

Since the first edition of *Management Teams*, the concept of team roles has spread world-wide. People have come to recognise types of executive behaviour that have a universal significance. The original Self-Perception Inventory (SPI) has been much used for this purpose but has now been superseded following further developments. Changes in the wording of the SPI have been introduced to take account of those for whom English is not a mother tongue. Two new scales have been added: a Control Scale embracing attractive items that carry no significance for teamwork, and a Specialist role. Most important of all, the views of others are now covered by Observer Assessments which link in with the SPI to give an overall picture of the candidate's team role profile.

A great deal of research has also been directed into jobs which best fit individuals with particular team roles and into the working relationships of those who work in close association with one another. The resulting complexity has created a need for computer processing, from which an expert, computer-based, system, called **INTERPLACE**, has been developed. INTER-PLACE, now in its fifth generation of systems, provides advice on a wide range of complex issues.

For more information and the current development status of **INTERPLACE**, please contact:

BELBIN
ASSOCIATES
The Burleigh Business Centre
52 Burleigh Street
Cambridge. CB1 1DJ
Tel: 01223-360895
Fax: 01223-368746